A WINTER
NAME *for*
GOD

A WINTER
NAME *for*
GOD

REFLECTIONS *for the*
CHRISTMAS SEASON

R. SCOTT COLGLAZIER

CHALICE
PRESS

ST. LOUIS, MISSOURI

Bible quotations, unless otherwise noted, are from the *New Revised Standard Version Bible,* copyright 1989, Division of Christian Education of the National Council of the Churches of Christ in the United States of America. Used by permission. All rights reserved.

Scripture quotations marked (NIV) are taken from the HOLY BIBLE, NEW INTERNATIONAL VERSION®. NIV®. Copyright © 1973, 1978, 1984 by International Bible Society. Used by permission of Zondervan Publishing House. All rights reserved.

"Try To Praise the Mutilated World" on page 79 is from WITHOUT END: NEW AND SELECTED POEMS by Adam Zagajewski, translated by Clare Cavanagh. Copyright ©2002 by Adam Zagajewski. Translation copyright ©2002 by Farrar, Straus and Giroux, LLC. Reprinted by permission of Farrar, Straus and Giroux, LLC

Cover and interior design: Elizabeth Wright

Visit Chalice Press on the World Wide Web at www.chalicepress.com

10 9 8 7 6 5 4 3 2 1   05 06 07 08 09

Library of Congress Cataloging–in–Publication Data

Colglazier, R. Scott, 1956-
  A winter name for God : reflections for the Christmas season / R. Scott Colglazier.
    p. cm.
  Includes bibliographical references.
  ISBN 13: 978-0-827242-50-6 (pbk. : alk. paper)
  ISBN 10: 0-827242-50-6
  1. Advent—Prayer-books and devotions—English. 2. Christmas—Prayer-books and devotions—English. I. Title.
  BV40.C54 2005
  242'.33—dc22

                                              2004030142

Contents

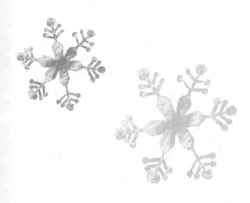

Introduction

Over the years I have grown to appreciate reading in snippets. Short bursts of narrative or brief essays give me a new thought or insight for the day. More specifically, I have become fond of reading a daily spiritual reflection. In some ways, it's just a good spiritual practice, but that's not really why I do it. I just enjoy it. Sometimes I keep a devotional book on my nightstand, or I have a book on my office desk and read from it each morning before I turn on my computer and begin answering e-mails.

This book, A *Winter Name for God*, is my attempt to offer some reflections during the Advent and Christmas season; moreover, it's a book that brings together some accessible thoughts on the Christian faith. They primarily consist of stories, experiences, and observations about life—the kind of life most often lived without fuss or fanfare. Nevertheless, I find the ordinary events of life often bring us the most profound spiritual insights about faith. I would simply point to the birth of Jesus as proof. An ordinary event from one viewpoint, his birth utterly changed the world.

This book is also about the human situation, especially our propensity to wander in the wilderness and live through winter seasons of barrenness and difficulty, grief and suffering. Where is God? What is happening to me? How can I believe in God while living in a world of cruelty and pain? This book is not a formal attempt to address such large issues, but I do offer ideas and practical suggestions for rediscovering God in the midst of our suffering.

Another reason for the book is a simple one—I love Christmas. I love the weeks of Advent that lead up to Christmas. I love the dark, brooding lectionary readings and the music of the season. I love being in church during the holidays, enjoying the light of hundreds of candles and participating in the wonderful spectacle of pageantry that defines Christmas. I even love shopping and selecting gifts for people. I'm moved each year by the quiet dignity of Christmas Eve, and then the explosion of joy on Christmas morning. I hope this book will nurture your spiritual life; I hope it will also enhance your celebration of Christmas.

You can use the book in various ways. As you can see from the format, it's meant to be read each day. Yet every chapter has a "stand alone" quality to it. Read what your soul wants to read when it wants to read it! One reminder: doing a reading each day is a great way of nurturing the spiritual life. I hope you will find a quiet place in your schedule to read one of the chapters (each of them can be read in just a few minutes), and then reflect on the message throughout the day.

I also think the book could be used in adult Sunday school classes or church study groups. A teacher might assign specific chapters to people, and then each one could kick off a conversation for the class. A good way to begin is simply to say, "One point that I liked, or what spoke to me, or what touched me was…" Start anywhere you like—usually, where you want to start is the place you need to start. Keep in mind the point of the book is not to give you new information about Christmas. The focus of the book is to take you deeper into yourself! The only way that happens is by reflecting, feeling, and praying. Take a little time for your spiritual life during December—your soul needs it!

Speaking of prayer, I also hope you will utilize the prayers at the end of each chapter. I wrote all of them in first person because I think praying is deeply personal. Feel free to adapt them to your own situation. It's easy to change an "I" into a "We"! You might want to do what I did while writing the book—read the chapter, reflect on it for a few minutes, then write your own prayer for the day, maybe just a sentence or two in a journal. There's something meaningful about writing out your own prayer.

My understanding of the Christian faith continues to grow and change, but one constant has been and remains the belief that God's love is revealed to the world through Jesus Christ. That love is the only thing that endures in life, the only thing that helps us make it through the winter seasons of our lives. In many ways, this book is my attempt to reflect and feel my way through a bleak period in my own life, trying not to give up on joy and love, and, more importantly, trying to believe that joy and love had not given up on me. I'm guessing I'm not alone in such an experience.

I take great consolation in the words, "For unto *you* a child is born." *You* indeed! He is born again and again to you and me, and most often we experience his presence when we least expect it (maybe when we have almost given up). The apostle Paul once wrote, "Love never ends" (1 Cor. 13:8). I still believe it is so. Therefore, each year I open my heart to the miracle of Christmas. I never know exactly what will happen or what part of the story I will need to hear as if for the first time, but without fail I discover new light for my darkness every Christmas. I find again a divine presence that endures with me through all my seasons. Therefore, I offer blessings to each of you, and, as always, regardless of *when* you are reading this, I wish you a Merry Christmas.

The Winter
of Bright Hopes

SECTION ONE

DECEMBER 1

Waiting for the Cherry Blossoms

*Beware, keep alert; for you do not know when the time
will come.*

Mark 13:33

We are all waiting for something to happen in our lives—the muddy waters of a relationship to clear, ominous test results from the doctor's office, an elderly parent to recover from surgery, a daughter to graduate from college, or even a sign from God indicating some *one*, some *reality* in the universe does love and accept us. The human experience constantly involves waiting.

The perennials we enjoyed in the garden a few months ago have now gone dormant under a blanket of snow. The great sugar maple trees stand bare as skeletons against a gun-metal gray sky. As for the days of winter, it's not so much that they have become shorter, but the nights have become longer. And so we wait, waiting for something to be revealed or resolved, waiting for something good to happen in our lives, and, perhaps most of all, waiting for God to answer our deepest prayers.

Waiting is winter business; it is God's business.

It fascinates me that on the first Sunday of Advent the lectionary scripture text for the church is about the *Parousia*, the second coming of Jesus to the earth. A passage such as Mark 13:32–37 reflects an early and pervasive hope that Jesus would quickly return to the earth, probably within the lifetimes of the first generation of Christians, and that he would establish the kingdom of God as a blessing for all people.

Regardless of what one believes about a second coming of Jesus, this much is true: the business of waiting is not easy. Our illusions, many of them long cherished, dry up and blow away while we experience our individual winters. Even the early church had to give up on the idea that Jesus would return quickly to the earth. Giving up an illusion, however, is not a bad thing. Just as winter lays bare the landscape, allowing us to see what might normally be hidden behind summer trees and vegetation, so our personal times of waiting help us see ourselves more clearly.

In the case of the early church, it meant they could not just sit around and wait for Jesus to show up and make the world better. They had to participate in the kingdom of God themselves by working for peace and justice and by sharing the good news of God's love with the world. The church had to find creative ways of waiting, the kind of waiting that translates into loving others and addressing the aching needs of people. Additionally, part of their waiting would require them to experience Jesus in a new way: not bodily—because he was no longer in their physical presence—but spiritually, discovering his influence in the midst of his absence.

Part of waiting is working for what you want to see happen in the world. But there's another part of waiting. It's the adventure of discovering the signs of God's presence in our world, signs that become like moths fluttering in and out of the branches of a California Live Oak at twilight. These signs remind us that we are not alone in the universe.

In Japan, hardly anything is more sacred than the blossoming of the cherry trees. Each year thousands of people fill the public parks and gardens to admire the delicate blossoms. People set up small tents and portable tables replete with flowers, food, and wine, all for the purpose of beholding the beauty of the cherry blossoms. It's a national party called *hanami*, literally the "viewing of the flowers." Adults wear their best suits and dresses; children run and play in the grass with their friends; and, of course, everyone captures the magnificence of the trees with a camera.

The Japanese are passionate about cherry blossoms. They enjoy cherry blossom rice cakes, ice cream, and tea. At one time in their culture a high school senior applying to a college would receive a letter from the university that simply read: *The Cherry Blossoms Are Blooming—Acceptance,* or *The Cherry Blossoms Are Not Blooming—Rejection.* What a wonderfully poetic way of doing business! But more than business, I think it's admirable that a culture would honor the simple act of watching the delicate beauty of the cherry trees.

Jesus' definition of waiting goes something like this: "Get ready to live! Prepare the world for God's joy! And don't forget to celebrate those moments in life wherein you encounter the divine presence."

His idea of waiting was similar to the Japanese holiday of *hanami.* He invited people again and again to wait for the blossoming of God, a blossoming even more voluptuous than that of the cherry trees. Waiting, of course, goes to the heart of the Advent season. On the one hand, we celebrate the first coming of Jesus by remembering his birth in Bethlehem. On the other hand, we prepare right now to discover his energy within our daily lives.

December is a perfect time to watch and wait. What are you waiting for during this Advent season? What will your eyes see this Christmas? The air is cold, and the earth is quiet; the world has once again shed its skin. Spring will come, as will the celebration of Christmas day; but it will not come too soon. Not before we have honored our human experience by watching and waiting for the presence of God.

Dear God, in all my waiting, in all my searching and longing, draw near to me. Give me patience to wait. To be still. To know that you are God. Open my heart to the stillness of your presence. Open my spirit to all that is unresolved, to everything that remains mystery and puzzle. And if it is possible, may something come to life during this sacred season, something beautiful and real. May the love of Christ be born in me and in your world. Amen.

DECEMBER 2

Finding the Missing Pieces

*But whenever you pray, go into your room and shut the door
and pray to your Father who is in secret; and your Father
who sees in secret will reward you.*

MATTHEW 6:6

I recently read a story that helped me understand what it means to be on a spiritual search. Paul Auster gathered a collection of personal stories from people throughout the United States into a book entitled *I Thought My Father Was God.*

The story I enjoyed the most was "Grandmother's China" by Kristine Lunquest. She writes about her parent's move to southern California from Rockford, Illinois, in 1949. They carried three children and all their earthly possessions, including four cartons of her grandmother's hand-painted china, featuring a distinct forget-me-not pattern. Unfortunately, something happened during the move to California, and one box of china never arrived at the house.

Kristine thus grew up in a household that had missing pieces of china—no cups or saucers or bowls. Every holiday meal her mother would partly laugh and partly lament the missing pieces of china. When her mother died in 1983, Kristine inherited the partial set of dishes.

She highlights a special Sunday ten years later in 1993. She crawled out of bed at 5 a.m. and headed to the Rose Bowl Flea Market in Pasadena. She walked up and down the aisles that morning looking for a few antique treasures. Just as she rounded the last corner, right before she left, she spied a table with some china on it. She picked up a cup and saw the unmistakable forget-me-not pattern. Right there were the missing cups and saucers and bowls. Yes, it was her grandmother's china.

Noticing her excitement, the dealer came over and eventually shared the story about how she had acquired the dishes. She purchased them from an estate sale in Arcadia, California, the little town where Kristine grew up. An unopened carton of dishes was found in a storage shed behind the house, where the owner said they had been forever. She was just trying to get rid of them because she didn't own the complete set.

Kristine Lunquest ends her personal moment of discovery with the following words:

> I left the Rose Bowl Flea Market that day laden with my amazing treasure. Even now, years later, I am filled with the wonder that 'all the pieces of the universe' tumbled together to let me find the missing china. What would have happened if I had slept in? What gave me the itch to go to the Rose Bowl on that particular day? What if I hadn't turned that last corner, choosing instead to leave and rest my aching feet? Last week I had a dinner party for 15 friends and used grandmother's china. At the end of the meal, I proudly served coffee in those beautiful cups and saucers that had been missing for so long.[1]

---

[1]Paul Auster, ed., *I Thought My Father Was God* (New York: Henry Holt and Company, 2001), 40.

It's a wonderful story, isn't it? It's wonderful because it speaks to what is often true spiritually in our lives: We find ourselves missing something. We may not know what it is or be able to articulate exactly how it feels, but we have an aching sense that something is waiting to be filled in our lives. I like the Advent season for many different reasons, but not the least of which is that it is a season of prayer. When I take time to pray, it often feels as if I am finding some of the missing pieces within my own soul.

We can go for days trying to handle things on our own. We can use our intellectual acumen to figure it out. We can use our psychological strength to handle stress or our financial resources to facilitate goals we wish to accomplish. We can even use our network of friends for support. Still the missing pieces only arrive when we pause and pray, opening ourselves up to the universe—indeed, to the presence of the Divine.

This is why Jesus emphasizes the inner dimension of prayer. We tend to emphasize the results of prayer, turning prayer into a divine mail-order catalog operation. For Jesus, praying is an inward movement. Prayer may change the world, but it happens only by changing us. Jesus never asks, "Did you pray enough?" or, "Were you sincere enough?" Such a view turns prayer into a human work of righteousness. Prayer never fails, because in our praying we move into our interior closets, inviting God's presence of peace and love to our lives.

Broadly speaking, you may think of prayer in two different ways. Perhaps using the image of light would be helpful. Every now and then I go to meetings where someone is using a laser pointer. With a red laser light you can point to what's on the board or projected on a screen. Some people think of prayer like a laser beam they are shining directly at God. But for me at least, I don't think of prayer that way. I pray not because I'm trying to beam something to or from God; I pray because I'm trying to find the missing pieces inside my soul.

You may also compare prayer to the little reading light beside my bed. It's not terribly bright, but it's enough light to read by at night.

One night I stopped reading for a few minutes. I looked down and saw the lamp's light had created a small disk of light at the place of my heart. That's an image of prayer for me. Not the laser beam focused at God, but the words I speak to God and the feelings I share in prayer allow for a softer kind of light to shine on the place where God most wants to live. Prayer's purpose is not to get things from God, but to open up a spiritual space with the divine Spirit.

For Kristine Lunquest, the whole experience of finding the missing cups, saucers, and bowls created feelings of amazement, wonder, and surprise as the "pieces of the universe tumbled into place." Let's face it; we have enough randomness in our lives to stop us from taking another breath. Yet the world is not all randomness. It's not all death and disease. It's not all winter! When the focus of our praying is giving thanks rather than acquiring things, we can begin to see life differently. Our world still reveals surprises of goodness and joy.

A prayerful paradox exists: By saying words to God, we lose the focus on ourselves. By losing focus on ourselves, we begin to find the missing pieces of who we are. I'm not sure what is missing in your life during this holiday season, but I encourage you to open your heart, to open your feelings and thoughts toward God's love. Some light will shine. And just maybe, maybe for you this Christmas season, the universe will tumble into place.

O God, something within me is both precious and fragile, strong and weak, whole and broken. For all that needs healing within me, come close and provide the love and compassion I need to be the person you created me to be. And for all that is missing, come close and provide the grace, the joy, and the peace I long to experience. I bless you during this winter season. Amen.

DECEMBER 3

Is It Ever Too Late to Return to God?

"Repent, for the kingdom of heaven has come near."

MATTHEW 3:2

An old woman lives in a farmhouse outside of Conyers, Georgia. She claims she receives direct apparitions and messages from the Virgin Mary. Years ago in the village of Chimayo, New Mexico, someone found a crucifix, held it to a pain-ridden leg, and suddenly the person was healed. Now, more than 30,000 visitors a year come to Chimayo. Many take home pinches of dirt, seeking to impart healing and health to their loved ones. In France, pilgrims travel to the little town of Lourdes to find a miracle. They face stifling summer heat or biting winter cold as they transport family members in wheelchairs or on crutches, all because they want a miracle from God. I think about these "miracles" and wonder to myself: Would an instantaneous, dramatic, utterly convincing miracle be enough to cause a person to return to God?

John the Baptist uses a particular word in his preaching. During the Advent season the church hears this word again and again. The word is *repent*. Although John spoke in harsh tones regarding repentance, the word embodies something exhilarating and positive. *Repent* literally means to take on a new mind or gain a new perspective. More than simply ceasing something bad, repentance beckons us to take on something good and move toward the positive in our lives. For John the Baptist, nothing was more positive than returning to God.

I suppose one can return to God in a variety of ways. One way that makes sense to me during this holiday season is to move toward God by returning to our dreams. Dreams are essential to our humanity. They reveal our most intimate spiritual longings and call us forward. They give us a sense of purpose that makes life worth living. Indeed, to live without a dream is to experience a spiritual winter. A blues song says, "stop pulling on the seams of my dreams." We all need dreams.

During the early 1800s in the infamous California Gold Rush, little mining towns sprang up along pristine California rivers almost overnight. Stores, houses, and saloons popped out of the ground like mushrooms after a spring rain. In many cases, once the mining boom in the area was finished, so was the town. They became known as ghost towns, places where empty buildings became monuments to a dead dream.

To be a human being is to breathe the oxygen of our dreams. We dream of a good career or financial success. We dream of writing a book, owning a business, or being accepted into an Ivy League university. We dream of finding our soulmate and enjoying a good marriage. We dream of shedding a few pounds and looking younger.

Despite the fact that dreams are essential to our souls, many of us stop dreaming. When we do, our lives become like little ghost towns. Who knows why we stop? Perhaps we've heard too many dream-killing messages: "You can't do that! You're not smart enough. That's never been done before. You're too old. You're too young." Over and over again we receive messages that undercut our lives, making us feel embarrassed and ashamed of our dreams.

One way we return to our dreams, and to God, is by recognizing that dreams must change. Just as we grow and develop as people, our dreams evolve too. Sometimes we have to find new dreams to replace old ones. It takes little faith to hang onto a dream that will never come to pass; it takes all the faith in the world to create a new one.

I saw an interview on *The Today Show* a few years ago with a family who had a child born with Down's syndrome. The mother talked about the many adjustments she and her family had to make because of this child. I admired her candor, because she didn't try to portray the situation any better than what it really was. Yet a fierce sense of hope ran through her words. I was particularly struck by the power of one sentence: "You know, we had to grieve the loss of a dream, the dream of a perfect child; but after we did, we now love this child more than ourselves."

Winter is a good time to mourn the loss of some of our dreams. It's also a good time to discover new ones. It takes faith (and not a little daring) to find new dreams for ourselves, but in the end it's always worth it. What new dream could you discover during this Christmas season?

What we need to help us return to God is not some super miracle from Georgia, New Mexico, or France. What we need is simply a little courage to dream again, to see that God is forever calling to us and that God is ready to breathe new life into the old bones of our disappointments. It's never too late to dream, just as it is never too late to return to God. Some days, especially during a personal season of winter, they can become one and the same thing. Dare to dream. Risk some faith. Your life is calling to you.

O God of all energy and imagination, too many times I find myself living a flat life, a life devoid of dreams and hopes for the future. I reach dead ends, not sure where to turn or what to do. I sense a call to move into the future, but I am often afraid to embrace it. I feel new dreams stir, but cannot see how they could come true. I ask today for simple faith. Not to know more or believe more, but for the capacity to trust in the possibility of new dreams. Amen.

DECEMBER 4

The Incredible Nearness of Life

For in him every one of God's promises is a "Yes."

2 CORINTHIANS 1:20

I am continually surprised at the number of people who think of miracles as supernatural invasions—that somehow God lives in the sky, drops down every now and then for a visit, and then rearranges the pieces of our lives. Of course, something within all of us wants this kind of God, and, in turn, this kind of miracle, especially when we find ourselves in a winter season.

Rather than thinking of miracles as divine interventions, we can think of them as incredible nearnesses. Michael Murphy has written, "A rolling thunder throughout the world, these incredible nearnesses."[2] Paul Tillich once wrote, "Anything that happens in the world that points you to the presence of God is a miracle."[3] The poet Walt Whitman joins the chorus by adding, "As for me, I know nothing else but

[2]Michael Murphy quoted in "Angels Among Us," *Time* (Dec. 27, 1993).
[3]Paul Tillich, *Systematic Theology*, vol. 1 (Chicago: University of Chicago Press, 1951), 117.

18

miracles…to me, every hour of light and dark is a miracle, every cubic inch of space is a miracle."[4]

The Advent season is a wonderful time to observe these divine nearnesses of life. And not merely to observe them, but to open the heart so they can be experienced with a depth of feeling and resonance. Rather than waiting for an invasion of God to fix our winter (a most human tendency, to be sure), our opportunity is to live fully into our winter, experiencing it by looking for those moments when the presence of God is manifest. Viewed in this way, winter is not a season we fight against, but one we passionately embrace with faith and courage.

Miracles can happen in a variety of ways. Surely one of the most important miracles that can ever happen is our *personal growth and development* as human beings. This involves not just doing the same thing again and again or having the same old reaction to the same old problem. It involves actually looking a little deeper into our souls and asking: "What is trying to happen for me, within me, and what is God calling me to learn today?" Anytime we learn and grow from an experience in life, it becomes a miracle.

Our *interactions* with people can also become miracles. Dan Wakefield has written, "I've learned that the most significant changes in my life, the empowering, enlarging, uplifting kinds of changes—the ones that seem like miracles—have come through encounters with other people."[5] It's amazing how life takes on a luminous quality if we will just pay attention to the gifts people bring us. Even in our most casual encounters with others we can find such miracles.

Expanding on this idea, I think we can also experience the miracle of *community*. What a strange concept it would have been at the beginning of the Christian faith for people merely "to go" to church. Church wasn't something one attended; church was an ecological system of relationships in which one lived. Too many of us have become

---

[4]Walt Whitman, *The Complete Poems,* ed. Francis Murphy (London: Penguin Books, 1996), 409.

[5]Dan Wakefield, *Expect a Miracle: The Miraculous Things That Happen to Ordinary People* (San Francisco: Harper SanFrancisco, 1995), 5–6.

religious tourists, attending church once a year (usually at Christmas, "whether we need it or not"), never experiencing the miracle of community. To be a participant in a community of faith is to experience the miracle of knowing and being known by others.

Another miracle is that of *presence*. I use this word because it's what I often feel when I think about God. I've never heard a literal voice of God, nor have I seen a miraculous invasion from on high. What I have experienced in my quietest moments, in my seasons when I felt disconnected from myself and from others, has been a divine presence of love and compassion. It is mystery. It is awareness that I am not alone in the world. Although I cannot prove this ineffable presence exists, I have felt it as an incredible nearness. For me at least, it is nothing less than a miracle.

In one of my favorite movies, *A Room with a View*, one of the characters, George, is too serious for his own good. Even on a wonderful holiday in Italy, he is riddled with cynical doubts and questions about life. Then he meets a young woman and falls in love. (Love is always a heart-opening miracle!) He doesn't know what to do with his contradictory experience. Tormented by his questions, he also feels as if the universe has given him this generous gift. His uncle, who is traveling with him, finally says, "You look at the universe, and all you see are question marks. But look a little closer, George, look a little more carefully; and if you do, you will also see that the universe is saying, 'Yes! Yes! Yes!'"[6]

During the Advent and Christmas season the church celebrates God's great yes to the world in the birth of Jesus Christ. The apostle Paul has written, "For in him every one of God's promises is a 'Yes'" (2 Cor. 1:20). I believe God is saying yes every day. Sometimes that yes is spoken as quietly as winter itself, the kind of miracle measured not in decibels but in depth of experience. It is the miracle of what we see, what we feel, and what we imagine. So during this season ask yourself:

---

[6]*A Room with a View,* directed by James Ivory, with Maggie Smith (Warner Homer Video, 1986).

"What is coming near to me?" The fact that we even find the courage to ask such a question suggests that an answer is near, closer to us than our very breath.

Help me, O God, to experience the quiet miracles of life. To grow and deepen my faith. To be aware of my interactions with others and to receive the gifts people bring me. To find true community by accepting others even as I risk sharing myself. And in those moments when I am alone with you, when the world has gone quiet and all that is left is the beating of my heart, help me to be touched by the miracle of your love. Amen.

DECEMBER 5

Awakening to a Beginning or an Ending?

Do you have eyes, and fail to see? Do you have ears, and fail to hear?

MARK 8:18

Several years ago while browsing through a bookstore with my children, we found an interesting book entitled, *The Magic Eye:* a book without any words or traditional pictures. Page after page is filled with detailed designs. Sometimes a series of dots covers the page. Other times you see a wild paisley pattern or a detailed print of gaudy wallpaper. The point of the book is that if you look long enough at each page, looking at it with a soft kind of focus, you can see three-dimensional pictures.[7]

---

[7]N. E. Thing Enterprises, *The Magic Eye*, vol. 1 (Kansas City, Mo.: Andrews and McMeel, 1993).

We purchased the book, took it home, and spent hours holding the book close to the nose, then holding it far from our eyes while closing and opening our eyes quickly in hopes of discovering each hidden picture. We wanted the magic to happen; but before it could, we had to learn a new way of seeing. Our seeing needed to become softer and more relaxed. The truth is we had to learn *not* to see. We also discovered that none of us could explain to anyone else how to see the 3–D pictures. As maddening as the book was (and it was for the first few days), when I finally saw the first 3–D picture, I loved it! I experienced the magic of seeing.

Advent is an invitation to see the world differently, if not magically. Not magic in the traditional sense of that word, but seeing the world with wonder and awe, seeing the working of God in the midst of a world filled with cruelty and violence. It's one thing to be able to name what is wrong with the world; it's quite another, however, to be able to find God's presence in the midst of everyday life.

Jesus once said, "They have eyes but do not see." Yet that could be said of all of us. What do you see when you see? What do you miss each day, not because it isn't there, but because you are simply not seeing the magic? Another way of asking the question is this: Where do you find the presence of Christ?

We might want to focus our celebration of Christmas this year, not so much on the literal birth of Jesus that happened centuries ago, but on discovering his presence in the here and now. The question isn't so much *Was* he born? or, *Is* he born? The question is *Will* he be born in us today? To find Christ in the present tense requires a certain kind of seeing. The poet e.e. cummings spoke about it as "the eye of the eye being opened." Eastern religions sometimes speak of the "third" eye. That's the magical way of seeing.

One of the most treasured Christmas stories is Charles Dickens's *The Christmas Carol*, about Ebenezer Scrooge and the transformation he experiences during the holidays. You'll remember that Scrooge had it "all," or at least from a certain perspective he had it all. He had hoarded an excessive amount of money, possessed more power than anyone else in town, and owned a thriving business in the face of a terrible economy. But Scrooge did not have friendship and joy, intimacy and love. Most of all, he didn't have himself.

One night on the mystical landscape of a dream, the Ghost of Christmas Past arrives and demonstrates to Scrooge the utter poverty of his life, how he had missed so much of his living because of his obsession with business and success. He missed his family. He missed having friends. He even missed his chance at true love. Throughout this nocturnal tale, Dickens utilizes the bleakness of winter as a literary symbol of the desolation existing within Scrooge's soul. Other ghosts appear—past and present. They rattle bones and shake chains in a graveyard to remind Ebenezer of where his miserly life is heading if he doesn't open his eyes.

When Scrooge finally awakens on Christmas morning, he is trembling and in complete panic. At first he believes he has reached the bitter end of his life. Much to his surprise, he has not reached an end at all, but a beginning. He has been given the greatest gift of life— a new way of seeing the world. He begins to live with zest and joy. He finds happiness in giving to others. He helps the poor, reaches out to his family, and most of all, discovers the true meaning of Christmas because he has discovered the essence of love. Suddenly, the world appears magical to Scrooge.[8]

Perhaps the spiritual life could be imagined like this. Each day is like turning a page from *The Magic Eye* book. We can see on the surface of life. Or, like the transformed Ebenezer Scrooge, we begin to see the deeper picture embedded within the day. If only we could see that Christ is in every gesture of human kindness. If only we could see that behind every disappointment is an opportunity and that, in spite of our mistakes and failures, each of us has something to offer the world. If only we could see that all endings, including the bitter, winterlike endings we experience from time to time, can become beginnings.

---

[8]Charles Dickens, *A Christmas Carol* (New York: Weathervane Books, 1843).

Thousands of years ago magi saw a star. It awoke something so strong within them that they began following it. They carried within their hearts hopes and fears, but also dreams for the presence of God in the world. They knelt before the child, the Christ child through whom God touched the world with love. If we have eyes to see it, the magic eyes of faith, the one who was born to them will be born to us.

Some days it's easier than others to see his presence. But every day, every page we turn offers us the opportunity to see again and begin anew. It requires faith as well as imagination, but what we see is finally up to us. Why not open your eyes during this holiday season? Why not open your heart to the magic that is life itself?

I pray, dearest God, not to have more but to see more, not to accumulate more but to experience more, not to do more but to be more. Increase my capacity to see below the surface of life, to witness the complexity and beauty of this world, and to know beyond all doubt that your mysterious presence pulses within all things. During this season as I prepare to celebrate the birth of Jesus, may a spiritual birth happen within my own spirit—nothing less than a birth of consciousness, awareness, and love. Amen.

DECEMBER 6

Creating the World We Want

For a child has been born for us,
a son given to us;
authority rests upon his shoulders;
and he is named
Wonderful Counselor, Mighty God,
Everlasting Father, Prince of Peace.
His authority shall grow continually,
and there shall be endless peace
for the throne of David and his kingdom.
He will establish and uphold it
with justice and with righteousness
from this time onward and forevermore.

ISAIAH 9:6–7

During the winter months, gardeners sit beside their fireplaces with catalogs in hand and begin to imagine the kind of gardens they will plant in the spring. They imagine red, lush tomatoes; purple, bulbous eggplants; row after row of fresh green beans; and maybe a little sweet corn to adorn the dinner plate come summer. Others of us imagine a July vacation, maybe a few weeks by the ocean, or perhaps a trip to the mountains of Colorado. One thing is for sure; before such an event happens, we first have to be willing to imagine it.

In much the same way, Advent becomes our opportunity to imagine the kind of world in which we would like to live. The Bible's prophetic tradition asks us to imagine a world of peace and justice, a world in which all God's children can participate in the blessings of life. This is why the Advent readings often refer to prophets such as Isaiah, Jeremiah, and John the Baptist. They represent God's hope for a better world. The kingdom of God is a vision of life and, therefore, a never-ending process of working for the well-being of others.

What would it mean for us to get ready, not just ready for another Christmas, but ready for a better world during this holiday season? What kind of world could you begin to imagine? What would it mean to practice more compassion toward others? What would it mean for us to restore the dignity of another human being, perhaps offering a graceful word, a kind gesture, or even some simple words of hope as this person endures winter? These are the questions we ask during Advent; these are the questions that prepare us, not merely for Christmas, but for Christ himself.

We can't wait until everything is perfect in our lives before reaching out to someone else. More to the point, sometimes the best way to lift ourselves up in life is by reaching out to someone else. If we can begin to imagine the world we want, then it simply takes courage on our part to implement it.

Go with me to the checkout line of a large grocery store. An older woman is one of the checkers. She's nice; but like all of us, she doesn't handle situations as patiently or humanely as she could. She is trying to take care of a customer who is a little unusual. Her hands are severely deformed, and she's really not very pretty. You can tell by looking at her that she is poor. She is doing her best to handle her groceries and baby.

After her groceries have been totaled, one of those completely awkward, fragmented scenes begins to unfold. Right there in front of the chocolate bars, breath mints, and gossip magazines, she doesn't have enough money to pay for her groceries. The cashier abruptly says to the young woman, "You don't have enough money." Because the customer doesn't hear very well, the cashier begins to speak more loudly, "You don't have enough money! How are you going to *pay?* You don't have enough *money!*" Everyone including God is watching, and everyone is completely embarrassed. The line behind the woman gets longer by the minute.

A friend of mine happened to be standing right behind the woman. He leaned over the counter and quietly said to the cashier, "Ma'am, just put her groceries with mine. I'll be happy to pay for them."

The cashier responded immediately, "No, you don't have to do that. She has to understand. She doesn't have enough money. She's got to *understand!*"

He said, "No, *you* don't understand. I want to do this. I really want to do this."

"You mean you just want to pay for all of them, all of her groceries?"

"That's right. I want to pay for all of them. I'll pay for the groceries."

Amid all this commotion, the woman next in line behind him jumped into action, "I want to help buy those groceries, too. I can help."

Someone else piped up, "Hey, I have some extra money. I can help."

Suddenly cash is flowing back and forth like a casino in Las Vegas. People are stepping up and reaching out, rallying around this young woman who was completely overwhelmed by her life circumstances, overwhelmed and embarrassed. The entire scene became one of those visible reminders that we have the capacity as human beings to bring a little dignity to one another. If we will just imagine it, imagine that it's possible, we can surely begin to practice it daily.

Not all the world's problems are so easily solved. We face challenges that continue to perplex and exhaust our compassion. We have no easy answers for terrorism and war, no simple solutions to poverty and homelessness. Yet the enormity of the problems should not paralyze our efforts to address them. During the season of celebrating the Christ child, it is good to remember what he ultimately stood for—the well-being of all God's children in the world. This is why we begin living today in a way consistent with what the kingdom of God is trying to become tomorrow. We may never fully reach it, but we will make a difference. I'm guessing that young woman in the checkout line would agree.

Before you go to sleep tonight, before attending one more church service or purchasing one more holiday gift, ask yourself: What can I do today to participate in the coming of the kingdom of God? Our individual actions will never eliminate winter's darkness, but they will bring a little light to the world. Some days a little light goes a long way.

O God, not only do I dream for a better life for myself, I also dream for a better world for others. Remind me that when one person is impoverished, I am impoverished. When one person is hurting, I am hurting. When one of your children in the world is diminished, so also am I diminished. During this Advent season, help me to prepare for Christ, not just for the beauty of his birth, but for the challenge of his mission in the world. Amen.

DECEMBER 7

The Music through the Fog

And suddenly there was with the angel a multitude of the
heavenly host, praising God and saying,
"Glory to God in the highest heaven,
*   and on earth peace among those whom he favors!"*

LUKE 2:13–14

A recent experience in California has become for me nothing less than a metaphor for how I understand the working of God. It had been raining all day—not just drizzling, but sheets of rain and hard-blowing wind pounding the West Coast. Such a storm makes you go to the window every few minutes and wonder if you shouldn't start building an ark! Finally, late in the afternoon it stopped raining. Desperate for some fresh air, I went outside. The air was cold, clean, and wonderful after the storm. I could smell pine and eucalyptus in the breeze as I walked down the hill toward the beach.

Along the coastline a large, billowy fog bank developed. It was thick and soupy, making it hard to see the ocean. I began walking on the beach—listening to the ocean and enjoying the sounds of crashing

aves. Through the thick fog, I started hearing peculiar sounds. I
ouldn't tell what they were or where they were coming from. I
ondered if it was the honking of a sea lion or maybe the sound of
ild geese flying overhead. I didn't know, but I kept walking along
he beach through the fog.

The further I walked, the clearer it became that the sound wasn't
oming from an animal at all—it was the earthy, guttural sound of a
agpipe. The further I walked, the louder the music became. I looked
p at the street above the beach but couldn't see anything. I tried to
ook ahead through the fog, but I couldn't see another person. I
ontinued walking and listening to the lilting music floating across the
each.

Then I saw him—a solitary bagpiper. A young man (I'm guessing
around 30 years of age), dressed in tennis shoes, blue jeans, and a tan
acket, stood on a large outcropping of rocks that jutted into the ocean.
Strapped to his shoulder was a magnificent-sounding bagpipe. I stood
till for several minutes and listened to his impromptu concert, deeply
ouched by this unexpected gift of music.

This image of music coming through the fog captures how I often
experience the presence of God. Faith teaches us, of course, that God is
always with us. It also teaches us that God is in all things. At the same
time, it's easy to lose sight of God's presence, easy to become lost in
our fog of grief or sadness, loss or anguish; easy to cry out, "My God,
my God, why have you forsaken me?" (Ps. 22:1a). Every human being
knows what it's like to endure a season of life when you question
everything, including God's presence. Yet faith has never been about
seeing; it's about trusting, especially trusting in those times when we
cannot see. Do you know what it is like to live in a fog?

In many ways, it's easy for me to think of Jesus as the music in the
fog. Through his remarkable life the music of love and mercy resounded
to the world. Some people during his lifetime heard it and responded
positively. Others did not. Some saw his music as foolishness, while
others treasured it like gold. Often the very ones who thought they
would never hear music again—the poor, the broken, the lost—heard

his music and followed it with the greatest of joy. His music affirmed the worth of all, promised that everyone could receive divine grace and announced that all people have a place and purpose in God's world.

Thousands of silent heroes live each day with courage and faith as they endure their personal winters. I marvel at women and men who find the strength to keep walking through disappointment, adversity, and illness. Maybe you are one of those people. Faith promises, of course, that if we will keep walking, even in the fog, we will find that ineffable presence we call God. More importantly, that presence will find us. Some days something beautiful happens, something so beautiful it catches us by surprise and becomes like music, music coming to us through the fog.

In the midst of a Christmas season we often find ourselves frenetically busy (busyness itself can become a fog), rife with unrealistic expectations. I wonder if it's possible for you to hear God's music? Is it possible to discover God's presence or see some sign of God's activity in your life? Is it possible to participate in your church with renewed enthusiasm and see that Christ is born there this year? Part of our watching and waiting during Advent is also listening, listening for those distinct notes of divine love coming to our lives. I wish you many days of good listening.

O God, you are the music coming to me each day. Give me new ears with which to hear and a new mind with which to think, and a new heart with which to feel. In the midst of this busy and demanding season, help me to hear again your song of love. As the angels shuddered with song, help me to feel again your divine presence. Help me know that I am not alone and that you are with me. And if it is possible, O God, may some song move through me to the world, a song of hope and love for all your children. Amen.

The Winter
of Discontent

SECTION TWO

DECEMBER 8

Living with Doubt in a Community of Faith

Then he said to Thomas, "Put your finger here and see my hands. Reach out your hand and put it in my side. Do not doubt but believe."

JOHN 20:27

Communities of faith should be places where people can talk openly—not just any kind of talk, but an exchange of ideas that constitutes meaningful religious discourse. It might seem obvious that a religious organization would want to talk about religion. However, after years of ministry in the church, I can assure you that church people focus a great deal of energy on anything but matters of religion. Often, organizational concerns and institutional survival become the obsessive focus, making it increasingly difficult for churches to actively participate in open and honest conversations about faith and culture.

Religious institutions harbor built-in conflict. Most of them were founded because people believed a particular religion provided answers about life. In some cases, people believed their answers were the *best* answers. In extreme cases, some tenaciously believed their answers were the *only* answers. Institutions like churches and temples and mosques are often looked to for an easy-to-read blueprint on how to live, or for explanations of the great issues of life and death and God.

Yet to turn religion into an easy answer is to diminish God as the ultimate mystery of the universe. The problem with religious communities trying to become the authoritative source of all answers is that not every answer will work for every person. People have minds of their own. Hearts too. We think and feel and experience life in our unique ways. What most of us need is not an institution to give us all the answers, but a place where we can ask our questions, a place where our most human explorations can occur without fear of recrimination or judgment.

This concept of being able to converse is important, particularly for those of us who have to face the reality of doubt within our faith. Faith and doubt are not mutually exclusive. In fact, just the opposite is true. We only doubt what we really care about; we only ask questions if we are interested. Therefore, in its own way, every doubt is an expression of faith; moreover, God welcomes and loves every person who has ever doubted. The problem many of us face is that the church often presents itself in a way that suggests doubts and questions are not welcome.

Safe sermons that never stretch the mind or challenge the heart lull church members asleep. Sunday school classes may appear open and friendly, but often it's clear certain questions and discussions are off limits. This creates a scenario within people of a deep sense of spiritual winter, people living alone with their thoughts because they're not really allowed to talk about thoughts and questions in their church.

During the weeks leading up to the beginning of the war in Iraq in 2003, a number of ministerial colleagues privately confided to me their ambivalence about the war, but few of them felt secure enough to share their thoughts with their congregations. I found no wavering in terms of support for the brave men and women serving in our military, only a concern about what it means to be a peacemaker in this particular global situation. Yet the idea of speaking about such an important topic felt too risky. Ministers feared such talk might somehow divide the church or be perceived as being less than patriotic.

Even from a national perspective, I cannot recall a time when ambivalence over national policy, let alone dissent, has been so quickly associated with a lack of support for the United States. Part of the greatness of America is that people can exercise freedom of speech, a freedom that goes to the heart of our democracy. This freedom, however, should be part of the fabric of faith communities, too.

Whether one supports this war effort or that military operation is not the issue. My concern is that religious communities are squandering critical opportunities to talk about important matters of faith and culture because they are afraid such conversations will damage the community or drive members away. Fear should never drive an organization, or, for that matter, a country. Fear should not drive a church. The topic could be the war, but that's only the beginning. Other pressing issues such as ethics and scientific research, cosmology and the new physics, the treatment of gays and lesbians within the church and our culture, and the very nature of the Bible itself challenge the church to provide robust conversations.

During this season of Advent and Christmas many Christians celebrate the certainties of their faith. Celebrating faith does not have to eliminate questions and doubts. In the end, what is important is not *what* we know but *whom* we know, and—most importantly—who knows us. Faith celebrates the loving presence of God presented to the world in the life of Jesus Christ, who knows each of us intimately. The church does not have to provide all the answers about matters of faith. The church can and should, however, be a place where ministers can freely preach about any topic. It should also be a place where individuals can sincerely ask their questions, express their doubts, and make their own connections about faith. A congregation does not always have to agree with their minister, nor does a minister always have to agree with his or her congregation! Both would be served well by fostering a healthy respect for meaningful conversation. Such conversation is essential to any religious institution, and, come to think of it, to any democracy.

What questions do you have about your faith? What parts of your faith make sense? What other parts have always bothered you? When is the last time you really spoke to someone about your faith, asking your questions and articulating your curiosities? One gift that would certainly be worth celebrating during this holiday season is renewing our faith by voicing some of our deepest questions about it. Simple graces are all around us if we will just open our eyes! Surely one of the simple moments we long for is finding a church that will let us be ourselves and that will encourage us to ask our questions. Under any circumstances, such a church would be a great Christmas gift.

Most loving God, I come to you during this important season of celebration, ready to affirm so much of my Christian faith, but also free enough to say that I have doubts and questions, some that have puzzled me for a lifetime. I ask not for simple answers, but for deeper questions. I ask not for quick solutions, but for more patience with all that nonpluses me. And in those moments when I live with more uncertainty than certainty, let me feel again your love for me in Christ. Amen.

DECEMBER 9

Christ or Cliché?

Her husband Joseph, being a righteous man and unwilling to expose her to public disgrace, planned to dismiss her quietly. But just when he had resolved to do this, an angel of the Lord appeared to him in a dream and said, "Joseph, son of David, do not be afraid to take Mary as your wife, for the child conceived in her is from the Holy Spirit. She will bear a son, and you are to name him Jesus, for he will save his people from their sins."

MATTHEW 1:19–21

The poet Robert Frost once wrote, "Something there is that doesn't love a wall."[9] I think the same could be said about a *cliché*. There is something that doesn't like a cliché. When they fly toward us like wounded birds in a storm, they trivialize our human experience and bring resentment instead of the healing that we want and need. They

---

[9]Robert Frost, "Mending Wall," in *The Poetry of Robert Frost,* ed. Edward Connery Lathem (New York: Rinehart and Winston, 1969), 33.

present truth without nuance or texture; everything is monolithic and one-dimensional. Unlike wisdom that is beautifully simple, clichés are completely simplistic, flat, and lifeless.

Religious clichés are especially painful because we turn to religion to discover meaning in the depth of our experiences. If all we encounter are clichés, then we are left feeling frustrated and bewildered, perhaps even questioning the legitimacy of religion all together. Not only do clichés undercut the true value of faith, they also undercut our experience as thinking, feeling human beings. This is especially true when something tragic happens in our lives. The last thing we need is a hackneyed cliché or overblown platitude about God.

I'm thinking about clichés because so much of what I hear during Christmas feels trite and superficial. I love Christmas and the numerous thoughts that break forth from this season of watching, waiting, and celebrating. What I don't like is when I hear Christ turned into a cliché.

I heard one not long ago during a storm of grief. A family had just lost their child to cancer. A beautiful young child, she remains to this day a part of my soul because of the courage and patience she exhibited while undergoing treatment. Standing in fellowship hall with friends and family after the service, I happened to overhear someone say, "I guess God needed her more in heaven than on earth." Sadly, that wasn't the first time I had heard someone utter those exact words.

Do you see how such words become a harmful cliché, how they miss the depth of hurt and loss these parents were experiencing? What does such a statement say about God? Does God cause children to die of cancer? Does God allow it? Is life only validated when one finally goes to heaven? Does God really need people up in heaven? I'm sure the person (doubtlessly sincere and well meaning) only made the situation worse by passing along such an idea. Perhaps it would have been better to acknowledge the family's grief, the senselessness of it all. Perhaps it would have been better to acknowledge not only the family's brokenness but also God's brokenness. After all, the winter name of God means God endures with us, not in an artificial way, but genuinely, because God knows the meaning of winter within God's own being.

Another cliché I hear often, particularly after a tragedy, is, "God is in control." A few years ago in Fort Worth, Texas, a terrible tragedy happened at Wedgwood Baptist Church. A mentally disturbed man walked into the church during a Wednesday night service and started shooting. He killed several young people before turning the gun on himself. This was an awful moment for the city, yet over and over again I heard ministers stand up and say, "My God is in control! My God is sovereign!"

Again, I'm sure they were well meaning, trying to assert the presence of God in the midst of a terrible tragedy. Nevertheless, it sounds like a cliché to me. God is in control? Well, if God is in control, why didn't God stop it? Why didn't God stop the Holocaust? Why didn't God stop 9/11? Why doesn't God stop the countless tragedies that happen each day throughout the world? And why didn't God stop the cancer from growing inside the little girl I knew?

I think God loves and aches for us. I think God has a certain kind of power in the world. But control? God's presence can be found in the midst of tragedy, meaning that new life can rise from the ashes of our lives and that death does not have to be the last word. Another way of saying it is that no experience stands beyond resurrection! (That's jumping from Christmas to Easter!) But God's presence is not a controlling, dictatorial presence. To suggest it is only passes along another shallow religious cliché.

In some ways, embedded in the Christmas story itself is the rejection of a clichéd way of thinking. When Joseph learned that Mary was pregnant, he, of course, was bewildered over how it all happened. He assumed she had been with another man. Still, he did not want to embarrass Mary (or, in that culture, possibly get her stoned to death), nor did he want to draw attention to himself. His plan, according to the gospel of Matthew, was to divorce her quietly. He was willing to do the normal thing, the clichéd thing, by sending her away.

God took Joseph beyond his surface thinking to the depths of the situation. God spoke to Joseph in a dream, moving him from conscious ways and patterns of clichés to a deeper, softer world of soul. His imagination was enlarged, and his heart opened a little wider. He learned that the child belonged neither to Mary nor to him, but instead belongs to God. One way to think about clichés is that they make the world smaller; one way to think about faith is that it makes the world larger.

We need to acknowledge that anything can be turned into a cliché: the flag; the cross; the Bible; the church; even Christ can become a cliché. Yet just as the first Christmas moved Joseph deeper into his situation, Christmas can also move us deeper and deeper into life. That means past the clichés of our faith and the platitudes we so often pass along to our neighbors. We can use language that empowers our spiritual lives, partly by not claiming too much for faith, and partly by not claiming too little.

Whether Christmas becomes a cliché or not is up to each of us. It requires us to use our imagination and think a little more deeply than we normally do. That is just a way of saying that it takes faith on our part. After all, if you can't exercise a little faith during the Christmas season, when can you?

Dear God, forgive me when I have chosen cliché instead of Christ. May the living presence of Christ—true love, true hope, true transformation—be born in me during this holiday season. After the wonderful dinner and presents and parties, may something real abide within me, something that is nothing less than the influence of the Christ in my life and world. Amen.

DECEMBER 10

The Face We Want to See

A voice cries out:
"In the wilderness prepare the way of the LORD,
    make straight in the desert a highway for our God.

ISAIAH 40:3

As the world becomes stark during the winter months, cold and knuckled down to the bone, we long for spiritual clarity in our lives. We ask questions such as, "Who am I?" and, "Where am I going?" "Should I stay in this job or make a change?" "Should my marriage be brought to an end?" "How can I best help my children?" "What can I do about my addiction?" Perhaps most deeply we ask: "Where is God in the midst of all my searching?"

The Advent readings for the church during December hold great irony. Many of the lectionary narratives take place in the desert (a geographical equivalent of winter), for precisely in the desert one can experience spiritual discovery. The desert cannot be avoided; nor should it be, for the desert harbors life. It is, however, a hard scrabbled experience to find ourselves in the desert. Some people, such as the unforgettable John the Baptist, intentionally move to the wilderness, seeking a spiritual renaissance. But most of us tend to go into the desert kicking and screaming, afraid of the amorphous demons that lurk inside our hearts.

The prophet Isaiah cries out, "Comfort, O comfort my people" (Isa. 40:1). But even as I hear these striking words each Advent season, either read from the lectern or sung by the choir, I'm reminded of how desperate we are for the elusive experience of comfort.

Two recent photographs in *The New York Times* continue to remind me of this poignant human need. The first was of the AIDS Memorial Quilt that had been unfurled in front of the Washington Monument. The quilt was eleven blocks long and consisted of 37,000 panels. Each panel represented a story of heartache and grief, not to mention courage and faith. Family members or partners had decorated each panel with items such as baseball caps, patches from favorite denim jackets, or little stuffed animals sewn to the squares. I don't think it's an overstatement to say that this quilt has become an icon of our national grief. The quilt places AIDS in its pandemic global context and thus utterly staggers our human imagination.

Having witnessed this momentous event one reporter wrote that for the most part, visitors to the quilt were as quiet as if they were at a shrine, with few sounds louder than sniffling, sobbing, and sighs. In the photograph you could see people milling around the quilt. Some were holding hands; some were hugging one another; and all of them, young and old alike, were looking for some face, some face of comfort.

The other photograph I'm thinking about was also taken in Washington, D.C.—on Veterans Day at the Vietnam Memorial. The day looked to be unusually cold and clear. The sun was shining, and the simple black wall of the Memorial glistened in the afternoon light. I couldn't quite tell how old the man in the photograph was (maybe in his late forties). He wore combat boots, a T-shirt, and a pair of camouflage pants and jacket. In the photograph you could see him standing next to the black wall with all those names, name after name after name. With outstretched fingers he touched the names as if reading

Braille. Was he looking for the name of a friend? Someone in his family? Maybe the name of his father? Or was he simply looking for the elusive gift of comfort?

"Comfort, O comfort my people," says God. Of course we need to hear God's comfort. We're as desperate for it now as ancient Israel then, while they lived in Babylonian exile. Ask any Vietnam veteran, and he'll tell you about wilderness. Ask any mother who has ever decorated one of those panels for the AIDS quilt, and she'll tell you about the desert.

Many of us want God to fix the desert—take us out and transport us to another place and time. In my experience, however, God rarely "fixes" the desert. God endures with us through a multitude of experiences, including the experience of our spiritual wilderness.

God says things to us like, "Take all the time you need. Be gentle with yourself. Don't be in such a hurry. You can linger with your grief or sadness or loneliness. I'm not going anywhere. Let's just sit down together." I imagine God saying to that mother kneeling at one corner of the AIDS quilt, "Be patient. I know your loss still hurts. I'll just mosey around until you're ready to go home." Or to that Vietnam veteran God says, "I'm not in a hurry. You stay here until you find that special name on the wall. I'll just sit over here on the bench until you're ready to leave." That's the comforting God of the Christmas season, the presence of God that is the face of love and compassion.

The movie *Dead Man Walking* starring Sean Penn and Susan Sarandon is the story of Sister Helen Prejean, a Catholic nun ministering to Matthew, a convicted criminal on death row. She walks with him on the way to his execution. He desperately calls to her, "Don't leave me! Don't leave me now, Sister. Don't leave me." She grabs his arm and continues walking with him—both in tears. Then she utters one of the most remarkable lines in the movie, "I want the last face you see on this earth to be a face of love."[10]

---

[10]*Dead Man Walking,* directed by Tim Robbins, with Susan Sarandon and Sean Penn (MGM/UA Studios, 1996).

As December moves us closer and closer to Christmas morning, surely this is the face we need to see, the face of love and hope, and yes, the face of God revealed to us in the Christ child. Regardless of the winter we may find ourselves in, a face appears to offer us comfort. With one look, one look of divine love, we recognize we are not alone. We have never been alone. Therefore, to all of you who find yourselves in the midst of winter this Christmas season, I would offer a simple word: Don't give up. Open your eyes. Keep looking. A face, a face of love, stands ready to reveal itself to you.

O God, I am searching for your face and presence. I am looking for the face of love. Forgive me for the many ways I have run from myself and from others and from you. Forgive me when I have turned away from the very things I have needed the most. In this season of watching and waiting, stay beside me as I continue my journey of faith. Amen.

DECEMBER 11

Flying Solo

"Look, the virgin shall conceive and bear a son,
*   and they shall name him Emmanuel,"*
which means, "God is with us."

MATTHEW 1:23

Not long ago while flying from Charlotte, North Carolina, to Dallas, I noticed a young man (probably 16 or 17 years old) sitting across the aisle from me. He wore typical hip-hop clothes: T-shirt, baseball cap, long sagging shorts, and Nike™ shoes. He looked pleasant enough, almost a cherubic kind of face; but on this early morning, he also looked tired and bored.

My eyes focused on a tattoo on the inside of his arm between his elbow and wrist. With no real artwork or design, it consisted of only one word. Even that word looked rather primitive, with uneven letters and amateurish scrawl. Since that day I continue to think about the word. The word was *solo*.

What moves a teenager to have *solo* tattooed on his arm? What feeling or mood was present when he walked into a gritty tattoo parlor and requested such a word to be scratched on his body for the rest of his life? Was he feeling all alone in the world, without friend or family or any kind of emotional support so critical to living? Was he feeling despair to the point that the word *solo* captured for him everything that had been defeated in his young life? Or was the word a sign of defiance? Something on the order of a radical statement against everything that could undo his future, a personal stand for his individuality in the midst of bedeviling influences? *SOLO.*

A certain trajectory marked Jesus' life, starting with his birth and going through to his resurrection. At his birth, Jesus is described as Emmanuel, "God with us." This is not only a profound statement about God's companionship with men and women; it's a summary statement of the Christian faith. God is about radical invitation and welcome. To have faith in Jesus Christ is to experience the companionship of God. As much as anything, the Christian faith is a proclamation that we are not alone in the universe. At the very end of his life Christ developed this same idea, "I am with you always, to the end of the age" (Mt. 28:20). From beginning to end, the trajectory embodied in the life of Jesus is nothing less than God's presence with human life.

Feeling alone and being alone are different. Being alone apart from other people is a natural part of life that comes and goes according to life's appointments. We can be alone and yet not feel alone. We all feel alone some of the time. Some of us feel alone all the time. A loss or some change in life may deliver the knockout punch and precipitate loneliness. On the other hand, the most insignificant of events can lead to loneliness. A mood of loneliness inexplicably descends upon us. We're not sure why or how it happened, but it stubbornly hovers within us like an overcast sky, seemingly without any external reason or explanation.

This kind of loneliness is woven into the fabric of our being. This is not the loneliness of what has happened to us, but of who we are as human beings. I have experienced this kind of loneliness most of my life. The more I talk about it with other people, the more I find many others have experienced it, too. Your life can be going along pretty well. You can have a nice job, a happy family, and a few dollars stashed away in the bank. An upbeat life doesn't stop a descent into this kind of loneliness. You can know people care about you and love you, but that doesn't create a firewall between yourself and loneliness. This kind of loneliness is like a low-grade fever. It's not daily, nor is it debilitating; it's just the nagging ache of being disconnected from life.

The Advent season is an opportunity to reconnect to our feelings, regardless of what they are. But if we only reconnect to our own feelings, we will have missed the gift of the season. We also have the opportunity to reconnect to our faith in Jesus Christ. Obviously, we live without the physical presence of Jesus, but we can experience another presence—his spiritual presence. In times of loneliness we are invited to know what we can't always feel, to feel what we can't always see, and to trust what is not always apparent—namely, that the presence of Jesus is with us.

Surprisingly, when we find the courage to sit with our loneliness and begin to actually feel it (as opposed to denying it or running from it), we begin to find that it's not as frightening as what we might have imagined. In the midst of loneliness God draws close to us. Sometimes a spiritual feeling renews our place in the world and gives us a new sense of peace. Sometimes the smallest of gestures opens up to us as the presence of God. A friend calls. A letter arrives. Or someone, perhaps a stranger on the sidewalk or a member of our own church, says just the word we need to hear. It may not eliminate our loneliness, but it touches us enough to remind us that no matter who we are or what we feel, none of us, none of God's children, ever have to fly *solo*.

Loving God, like a mother you sit with me through the night when I am restless and anxious. Like a father you search for me when I am lost and alone. In my moments when I am alone and feel alone, I ask that you come close and comfort me. Help me move into myself more deeply, embracing all that grieves and hurts. But also help me move out of myself, learning to love others even as you have loved me. Amen.

DECEMBER 12

Apart, but Together in Heart

For we are the temple of the living God; as God said,
"I will live in them and walk among them,
*   and I will be their God,*
*   and they shall be my people.*

2 CORINTHIANS 6:16

Does any emotion pull harder on the heartstrings than wanting to be home for Christmas? But it's not just during Christmas that we miss people! Indeed, one of the most common winter experiences we can endure is living apart from the people we love.

Not long ago, I discovered a little Internet Café in Paris where I could purchase a card allowing me allotted time on one of their computers. The business was clean, brightly lit, and open 24 hours. People of all ages and nationalities came there. In a certain way, that little Internet Café became my touchstone for everything that was back at home.

One night in particular while responding to several e-mails, I noticed a woman with dark, sharp features sitting next to me. I'm guessing she was in her mid-50s. She read her messages and furiously typed responses while tears streamed down her face.

After about an hour, the pastor in me had about all he could take, so I leaned over and asked if she spoke English. She responded with a bright, "Yes."

"I don't mean to intrude, I explained, "but I noticed you were crying. I'm wondering if you're all right."

She laughed and wiped away her tears. "Oh, it's my family," she said. "I'm reading all their e-mails, and I miss them so very much." She explained that she was from Italy but living in Paris for a month. She went on and on about how homesick she was feeling.

"Why don't you go home if you miss your family so much?" I asked. "You could be back in Italy in two hours."

She replied, "Oh no, I can't do that. I *need* to be here right now." She never elaborated on why she needed to be in Paris, nor did I think it was my place to ask. But her words possessed amazing backbone and resolve—"I *need* to be here right now."

At one time or another each of us is separated from the people we love. A son might live in New York while a daughter resides in Seattle. A mother might live in Kansas while a dad lives in Florida. Or our children marry and have their own families. Often they make holiday plans to visit the other side of the family, and that means separation. This sense of separation happens with friends, too. All it takes is a familiar voice on the other end of the phone announcing, "I wanted you to know I've accepted a new job and will be moving in a few weeks." Of course, the most difficult separations occur when a loved one dies. A friend recently confided to me after her mother's funeral, "The hardest part is knowing I will never be able to pick up the phone and call my mom again."

There's no easy way to live with these winterlike separations. Yet a little spiritual perspective might help. It can make an enormous difference to trust that people can be spiritually connected even when they are apart. The most important connections we share are inner connections, unions of heart, feelings, and consciousness. This is why almost every world religion emphasizes that as long as people are remembered in our minds, they somehow remain in our hearts. One of the hardest lessons the early church eventually had to learn was that, although Jesus was no longer with them physically, he nevertheless remained with them in a new spiritual way. The same is true with the people we love; they may not be before our eyes, but they can always be present inside our hearts.

We also have to learn to be connected without being attached to one another. It takes enormous courage to stay connected to another human being, even while letting go of our need to grasp or control. Some of us confuse attachment with closeness. True intimacy always gives the other person room to breathe and become. An insight from the book of Philippians has been helpful to me. Speaking of the eternal Christ, Paul writes that he "did not consider equality with God something to be grasped" (Phil. 2:6, NIV). Even within the complexity of God, there is the practice of nonattachment. I simply mean that Christ, at least according to Paul, could have remained attached to the heavenly comfort of God, but instead chose to let go, to empty himself in loving devotion to the world. In this sense, all of life is an evolving process of loving and letting go.

The people we love often need to be away. They are on a sacred quest to become the human beings God created them to be. That's why we move a child into a college dormitory to begin the freshman year. They need to be away to grow. Love is not smothering people with fearful intensity. It requires us to let go and embrace absence as well as presence.

Christmas is a time of great emotion and longing. Of course, we miss our loved ones during this time of year. I'm wondering if you are missing someone right now, maybe this year more than any other Christmas. I've thought a great deal about that woman in Paris who said, "I *need* to be here right now." Even though she and her family were separated by miles and clearly missing one another, they seemed to be connected at the spiritual center of the heart. At least that's how I choose to remember those tears falling from her eyes.

I hope for you the literal experience of being with the ones you love during this Christmas season. But if that is not possible, I hope for you many good and wonderful connections of the heart, knowing and feeling that though apart, people can still be together. It's the power of memory, faith, and imagination. And not to be underestimated, it is the power of Christmas itself.

Loving God, although I do not see you and hear your literal voice, I still believe I am intimately connected with you in my heart. I miss loved ones and friends, especially this time of year when so many families seem to come together. I ask that you will help me treasure my family and friends, treasuring experiences and memories, and help me to be grateful for how our lives have intersected through the years. Teach me the lesson of holding others in my heart during this holiday season. Amen.

DECEMBER 13

Making Our Way Home

And the Word became flesh and lived among us, and we have seen his glory, the glory as of a father's only son, full of grace and truth.

JOHN 1:14

On the corner of West 79th Street and Amsterdam Avenue in New York City sits a restaurant called the Homesick Café. That strikes me as such a lovely, albeit lonely, name: *Homesick Café.*

Home, of course, is an elusive concept. It's more than a house, and certainly transcends a literal street address. Home is a feeling that rises up within us the way wild roses climb fence rows on Cape Cod, releasing their fragrance early in the morning after a rain. Sometimes the feeling of home is tied to a place, like a hometown or an annual vacation destination; but often the feeling of home transcends the familiar.

Here's what we know about home: Experiencing it is always wonderful; not experiencing it makes us homesick until we do.

Not long ago I went through the excruciating experience of having a kidney stone one Thursday night. The stone exited—finally—my body on Sunday morning. That same afternoon I boarded a plane for Asheville, North Carolina, where I had been scheduled for more than three years to speak at a conference. I was in North Carolina for three days and felt perfectly miserable the whole time. I was exhausted, running a slight fever, and still taking pain medicine. I would make a presentation at the church, only to return to my hotel room to sleep until the next scheduled event.

The highlight of the week came when a friend of almost twenty years dropped by to see me. It was great to see him. Seeing Wayne Hillis that day was like finding a little bit of home. We talked. We laughed. And, of course, I told him about my kidney stone! He then said something that resonated so deeply within me that I could barely hold back my tears. He said, "You know, when you're sick, there's only one place you want to be, and that's home." Suddenly, as when I saw the Homesick Café in New York, I knew it to be true—there is no place, no place, quite like home.

The gospel of John says, "And the Word became flesh and lived among us, and we have seen his glory, the glory as of a father's only son, full of grace and truth" (1:14). Interestingly enough, this same passage could also be translated, "And the Word became flesh and pitched his tent among us." This suggests that in the life of Jesus God made a home among us. Not only did God make a home, but in the amazing life of Jesus Christ, God made an offer for us, for our drifting, aching, lonely human spirit to come home.

Part of what the church embodies is a living home for people. Paul reminded the church at Ephesus (primarily Gentile in background) that at one time they had been strangers and aliens, far from the blessings of God. But now in the life of Jesus Christ they had been brought near. At last, they had come home to God. (See Eph. 2:19.) It's no coincidence that one of Jesus' most memorable parables is the story of the prodigal son. His homecoming is so memorable because within each of us is the memory and hope of home, home with God and home with ourselves. We are restless until we find both.

When I walk past the *Homesick Café* in New York, I always feel a little sad because it reminds me that home is so hard for some of us to find. I think that's especially true during the Christmas holidays, even though the idealization of home is pervasive. Missing home, however, may well be the first step toward finding home, a home that is not an address or house or town, but a spiritual connection with the one who pitched his tent among us. God's presence is always a place of love and acceptance, forgiveness and compassion. It's always the place where we belong.

During this season when so much is made of "going home for Christmas," I hope you will know that home has come to you. We name that home variously with words like God and Christ and Holy Spirit. But in the end there is only one name that counts. It is the name of love. Surely love is what Christmas is about.

In me, dearest God, something wanders homeless and alone. Yet I want to be at home with you, with others, and with myself. I am grateful that in the life of Jesus Christ you have come home to me, demonstrating that love is always to be my home. You have become for me father and mother, brother and sister. Just as you have welcomed me home to yourself, I ask that you will help me to embody your welcome to others. Amen.

DECEMBER 14

The Walking Wounded Are Welcomed Home

And she gave birth to her firstborn son and wrapped him in bands of cloth, and laid him in a manger, because there was no place for them in the inn.

LUKE 2:7

William Trevor's novel *My House in Umbria* does not mention Christmas even once. Yet I find myself thinking about this remarkable book as the Christmas holiday draws nearer. Set in the beautiful Italian countryside, the novel features Emily Delahunty, a romance novelist. Riding a train from Florence to Rome, she carefully notices the people around her. A young German couple tenderly touches one another. An American mother and father travel with their two small daughters. An older man sits beside his grown daughter.

A bomb explosion suddenly shatters their routine trip. Glass flies. Screams fill the air. The train rips apart and comes to a screeching halt.

Only four people survive this random act of violence—Mrs. Delahunty, the older man, a German, and one of the American girls. They are rushed to the nearest hospital, where they recuperate for many weeks from severe burns and lacerations.

When the time comes to be dismissed from the hospital, the only place they have to go is Mrs. Delahunty's villa in Umbria. She graciously invites her fellow survivors to stay with her until they have completely recovered. Remembering that day, she reflects, "We were all dismissed on the same afternoon, and the first night in my house we sat around the tiled table on the terrace...a stranger would have been surprised to see us, with our bandages and plaster, the walking wounded at the table."[11]

In many ways, when I think about the first Christmas, I think of the walking wounded. Mary was utterly bewildered over the news that she would carry this child in the hollow of her body. Joseph experienced the indignity of having to spend the night in a barn because there was no room in the inn. The shepherds were crusty and weather-beaten. The magi brought extravagant gifts of gold, frankincense, and myrrh, but were inwardly tortured over the demands of King Herod to spy upon the child. Even after the birth, the Holy Family had to flee their home to escape what has been called the "slaughter of the innocents."

The presence of the walking wounded at the birth of Jesus reveals something of the profound truth of Christmas itself. Christmas means that God welcomes the walking wounded home. Just as the poor, the broken-hearted, and the discouraged surrounded the child at his birth, so today women and men with all their sins, foibles, and differences are invited to make their way home to the table of divine grace. I can't help but wonder: Has there been something that has wounded you this past year?

---

[11]William Trevor, *My House in Umbria* (New York: Penguin Books, 1991), 35.

Some Christians seem to be preoccupied with deciding who is acceptable to God and who is not, or who should be included and excluded at the table of life. Such a religious emphasis is a terrible waste of time. Moreover, it betrays the essence of where Christianity started— an obscure barn, a miraculous birth, and the welcoming declaration of "Peace on earth and goodwill to *all*."

That we continue to have the walking wounded in our world is clear enough. As a nation we continue to experience repercussions from the attacks on the World Trade Center. We have been a nation at war, accumulating more and more losses, not only literally for families, but losses in our stature as Americans throughout the world. Every 14 seconds a child is orphaned somewhere in our world because of AIDS. Each year more than 16,000 deaths occur on American highways because of drunk drivers. Americans continue to experience what some psychologists are now calling an epidemic of depression. Truth be told, there is no end to listing the wounds of the world.

For Christians, the observance of Christmas can be a wonderful time of celebration and worship. Like others, I look forward to spending time with family and friends; and, of course, I love being in church on Christmas Eve. But it's also a time to reflect on what made Christmas worth celebrating in the first place, namely, that all were welcomed at the table of God.

I believe God welcomes everyone home. For me, at least, that's the essence of Christmas. We have good news, even in the midst of winter. That news can be articulated in a variety of ways and voiced with a multitude of words. But, finally, the Christmas story comes down to this: No matter who we are or the kind of winter we are experiencing, we are all welcomed. God especially welcomes the "walking wounded." So, my encouragement to you today is simple: Don't let your wounds stand in the way of Christ. Instead, allow Christ, and this community of Christ we call the church, to touch your wounds during this sacred season.

Dearest Lord, help me during this season of welcome and celebration to make my way to your table, finding again your goodness and love and grace. And help me to welcome others, too, believing that all your children can find a place in your presence. Help my church to be a place of welcome, real welcome—not just words but honest acceptance and friendship. I offer this prayer in the name of the Christ child who welcomed all at his glorious birth. Amen.

The Winter
of Divine Grace

SECTION THREE

DECEMBER 15

The Anguish of God

"For God so loved the world that he gave his only Son, so that everyone who believes in him may not perish but may have eternal life."

John 3:16

No doubt about it. Our suffering causes us to question the working of God, even to the point of wondering where God is in our lives. But there's another kind of suffering, not the kind we experience personally, but observable suffering. We watch the evening news and hear of horrendous acts of violence, such as suicide bombings in the Middle East or racial violence in the United States. Or maybe something happens in our own town, making us question what kind of people we are and what is happening to our world.

Not long ago, sitting in my office early on a dark and rainy morning, I looked out the window and noticed a soft, peachy gloom had gathered around a street light. I was trying to write the first sentence of a sermon. On that particular morning, I would have been happy with anything—a simple necklace of nouns and verbs strung together to get me started.

Then I wrote this sentence: "We live in a random universe where anything can happen at any given moment, and to think differently is to kid ourselves." I immediately hit delete!

I deleted it because I didn't like it. I still don't like it. I don't like it because I don't want to believe it. It's not the world I want, nor is it the world my faith has given me. I want to believe the world has rhyme and reason, that A leads to B and B leads to C.

I sat at my desk another thirty minutes drinking my latte from Starbucks. It tasted the way it's supposed to taste, tasted the way it did yesterday and the day before and the day before that. I had read my newspapers that morning, taken a shower, brushed my teeth, and combed my hair. As far as I knew, my kids were safe and happy. Yes, I wanted to believe that the many pieces of my world were in place.

Yet in the face of all that seems reasonable, the world does not unfold in an orderly way. A bus driver in Maryland, for example, waits at the corner for his first passenger of the morning. Randomly, senselessly, a sniper's bullet rips through his body. A bus driver who may have read his morning newspapers, took a shower, brushed his teeth, and combed his hair; a bus driver who, for all I know, stopped at Starbucks and ordered his own latte, just as I do every morning, was shot and killed. His name was Conrad Johnson.

"We live in a random universe where anything can happen at any given moment and to think differently is to kid ourselves." This time I didn't delete it.

After 9/11 a New York City family wanted a safe environment and so moved to Colorado. They were driving in their minivan. Suddenly, a large steel beam installed on an overpass a week earlier began to bend, yawning downward toward the road until it just snapped like a rotten tree branch during a thunderstorm. The beam crashed down at just the perfectly wrong, random time. It landed on top of the minivan, and this safety-seeking family was killed instantly.

"We live in a random universe where anything can happen at any given moment and to think differently is to kid ourselves." I can hit the delete button or not, but it won't change a thing for this family.

I think about boyhood days when I was frightened by Alfred Hitchcock's movie *The Birds.* I now realize that Hitchcock was making an important paradigm shift regarding evil and suffering. You could be walking along the beautiful shores of Bodega Bay in California, and inexplicably, randomly, out of the literal blue, a bird could attack you and not just one bird, but many birds. No rhyme. No reason.

For centuries people believed that evil had an address, complete with house numbers and a five-digit zip code. This is how the whole concept of *the* devil came into being; it was a way of pinpointing evil. "Why did this happen?" "Oh, the *devil* did it." Hitchcock skillfully raised a different question: What if evil is nonlocatable? What if evil happens randomly, capriciously, without respect to person or place? What if evil and suffering is broader, deeper than what anyone can imagine? More to the point: How do we live, how do we have faith in God while living in a world that seems utterly random?[12]

If God has a grand plan for people, it's hard for me to see it. If evil is only apparent and not real (as people of faith often claim), then it's hard for me to believe it. I'm left trying to make sense of a world that from all appearances is random—littered with violence, accidents, and disease—random with our human propensity to harm one another. To experience such capriciousness in a personal way is a winter season, to be sure, but to observe it in the lives of others is also a kind of spiritual winter.

The best I can do is this: I believe in the kind of God that invites goodness in people. God doesn't make people become good. God doesn't stop bullets from killing people. God doesn't catch steel beams before they land on minivans. I believe in a God who will give comfort and grace to the family of Conrad Johnson as they continue to grapple with his senseless death. I believe in a God who will be with people when they start their cars in the morning and pull out of the driveways. Moreover, I believe in a God who is anguished that two little boys will

---

[12]*The Birds,* directed by Alfred Hitchcock, with Tippi Hedren and Rod Taylor (Universal Studios, 1963).

not see their father again or that an entire state will grieve over a family wanting a little peace and safety in Colorado. And I still believe in a God who inspires compassion and beauty. In spite of the worst of our humanity, something profoundly good about life still exists. In this sense, there is something amazingly strong about God, but also something tender and vulnerable.

I cannot delete what is at least one side of the truth: "We live in a random universe where anything can happen at any given moment, and to think differently is to kid ourselves." That truth was made clear just after the birth of Jesus when Herod initiated his slaughter of the innocents. None of the parents of those infants could have seen it coming. But randomness is not the whole truth; at least I hope not. God offers God's self to the world, tenderly and beautifully. God waits for a human response. Even when our response is less than what it should be, God pushes aside anguish and hurt, enduring with us because, well, because that's how love works.

I suppose that's why I look forward to Christmas each year. Without fail, something happens in our world during the Christmas season that sobers us, that reminds us there is an inescapable randomness to life. At the same time, the story of the Christ child communicates to us that God's presence is both tender vulnerability and strong love. It's just the thing a person needs to remember in the midst of winter.

I open my eyes to the world, O God, and often I am overwhelmed by the suffering I witness. Not my own, but the suffering of others. I cannot begin to imagine the anguish you must feel as you see our inhumanity and watch our tragedies unfold. During this season as I come closer and closer to the birth of Christ, I ask for peace in the hearts of all your children. Amen.

DECEMBER 16

The Healing of Scars

But he was wounded for our transgressions,
  crushed for our iniquities;
upon him was the punishment that made us whole,
  and by his bruises we are healed.

ISAIAH 53:5

A couple of years ago I opened the oven door to baste the traditional Thanksgiving turkey. Instead of pulling it out, I reached my hand into the oven, dipped a spoon into the pan, and attempted to ladle the juices on top of the bird. That's when it happened. The top of my right hand hit the oven element—just for a split-second—and I burned my hand. That small meeting between my skin and the oven turned into a one-inch long painful burn.

For the first couple of days, it didn't look like much of a burn, just a darkened mark on the top of my hand. After a few days it started to blister, almost like it had been burned from the inside out. The burn began its ugly transformation into a grotesque-looking sore that I covered with a bandage. I applied ointment on it regularly and left the bandage off, thinking fresh air would help. Eventually it started to heal, but as it healed it started to itch and developed a scab. I accidentally knocked the scab off several times. This cycle went on for weeks.

What I noticed, however, is how self-conscious I became about the burn. People would stop me in the hallway at church and say, "Oh, what did you do to your hand? That looks terrible!" When I shook hands with people (remember it was my right hand), I could see them looking at my burn. If they didn't say anything, I knew they were wondering what happened. I performed weddings for couples while it was healing. I noticed the bride and groom looking at my right hand as I handed them their wedding rings.

I especially noticed it on Sunday mornings. During the Advent season people were coming forward to receive holy communion. Each Sunday as I held the chalice and people came close me, I could see them looking at the burn on my hand. I was supposed to be concentrating on the eucharist, but during those four Sundays all I could think about was what other people were thinking about when they saw the burn on my hand.

I'm not the only one who has ever felt self-conscious about scars. We all have them, don't we? Life has scarred every one of us. Sometimes our scars are self-inflicted. We make stupid mistakes, and the consequences scar us. Other scars are not of our choosing. Someone hurts us or abuses us, perhaps even when we were children; and we spend a lifetime learning how to live with our scars. Still, other scars just happen, and it's really no one's fault. They happen because we were in the wrong place at the wrong time.

Scars on our skin are not nearly as painful as the ones inside our lives—the lost job, the broken marriage, or the child who got in trouble last weekend with the police. Maybe it's the suicide of a brother or the illness of a mother or the lost investment that set us back financially. Life has scarred us all.

What scars are you carrying?

Mary, the mother of Jesus, would probably say God specializes in helping people learn how to live with their scars. Remember her reaction on hearing she would have a child? In Luke, chapter one, Mary sings a wonderful song, commonly called "The Magnificat." She begins, "My soul magnifies the Lord, / and my spirit rejoices in God my Savior, / for he has looked with favor on the lowliness of his servant." She goes on to sing of the God who has "lifted up the lowly," of the God who "has filled the hungry with good things," of the God who "has helped his servant Israel."

Mary understood what so many of us struggle to understand: Wounds and scars do not get in God's way. They may get in our way, but pain and failure do not get in God's way because God is moving toward us each day. Some of us think God *can't* love us because of our mistakes. Just the opposite is true. God loves us *especially* because of our human scrapes and burns.

It would be hard to determine the biggest misconception about the church. Surely one is that people only turn to religion because they are desperate and having problems. That happens from time to time; but after years of ministry within the church, I can safely say that people usually stay away from religion when they are hurting the most. Instead of turning to God, they withdraw and cut themselves off. Instead of seeking a new beginning, they stay away from the church— embarrassed or afraid everyone is staring at their scars.

Mary was granted an eternal glimpse into the essence of God when she learned that God had blessed her—a young, peasant girl—with the Christ child. Her glimpse is available to all of us. When you finally unfold the Christmas story, you see a God who draws near to us, especially to those of us scarred by life.

I hope you will see for yourself during this Christmas season that there is no wound God cannot heal and no scar that will ever turn God away from you. That does not mean God will prevent our wounds or eliminate our scars. That's not how God works. I hope each of us can discover that, even with our many scars, God continues to love us.

I hope you will also discover people who are willing to overlook your scars, who don't really care whether or not you're perfect. The people I'm thinking about are called the *church*. The church has a lot of aults, but it can also bring healing to our lives if we'll just give it a chance. It's a place to worship, a place to think and feel and share. It's a community that will care for us. The church heals us in quiet, imperceptible ways that we don't even understand. That's what I thought about during that memorable Advent a few years ago as I suffered through several weeks with a burned hand. By the time Christmas Eve rolled around, I was surprised that I could barely see my burn; I could barely see even a scar.

In so many ways and at so many different times, the church community has healed my life. The church can bring healing to your life, too. What's so amazing is that the healing happens slowly. It occurs so subtly we barely know it has taken place until we happen to notice one day that we are smiling and laughing again, or that we have made new friends, or that we feel the presence of God. Sometimes you look down and see a faint scar on top of your hand, and you can barely remember how it got there.

I bring my scars to you, O God, believing that you will not turn away from me. Some of them are my own doing. Others have accumulated over a lifetime. For all that I am, and all that I am not, and all that I hope to be, I ask your love and blessing. Thank you for the church. Although it is not perfect, it has been for me a place of love and acceptance. Inspire me to share your healing love with others. Amen.

DECEMBER 17

Trying Harder Isn't Always the Answer

> *For by grace you have been saved through faith, and this is not your own doing; it is the gift of God—not the result of works, so that no one may boast.*

EPHESIANS 2:8–9

Some of us received the following messages loud and clear as children:

"Work hard."
"Try your best."
"Give 100 percent."
"If at first you don't succeed, try, try again."
"Don't ever give up."
"Full steam ahead."
"Give it your best shot."
"You won't know until you try."

"Everybody loves a winner."
"Failure is not an option."
"You need to have willpower."
"God expects the best from you."

If by chance life didn't turn out the way we wanted, then we had only one solution—"Try harder!" I was brought up in the school of "try harder," and I'm guessing some of you were too.

Trying harder often characterizes the Christmas season. Shopping has almost become a full-contact sport during December. If we try harder, we'll find the perfect gift for that family member or friend. If we try harder, the Christmas dinner will be perfect this year, and everyone will be happy. If we work at it a little more and organize our schedule more effectively, then we'll be able to attend all three holiday parties over the weekend. If we just try harder, then maybe we'll be happy, not to mention satisfied and fulfilled.

For many people, the month of December is a brutal survival test. We find ourselves trying to manage event after event, spending endless amounts of money (or so it seems), and traveling here and there amid our obligations to work, family, and friends. We may sing "Silent Night, Holy Night," but the reality is very little is silent during the Christmas season. If we do discover silence, it's often in the utter exhaustion we feel as we slump into a chair and think to ourselves, "Is this really what Christmas is all about?"

Part of the beauty of Jesus Christ is that he embodies grace. Grace isn't about trying harder, nor is it about achieving and earning and deserving something. Most of all, it's not about being worthy of anything. In the end, grace is letting something come close to us, allowing God's grace to move toward us. In this sense, grace is like poetry in motion—pure gift and, therefore, pure joy. You can always tell when you're in the presence of grace because what you feel is a sense of wonder and surprise. It may not be a literal surprise, but it feels like a surprise in our hearts.

I spend a great deal of time each year in Carmel, California, where I go to write, to read, and to reflect. There I feel as if I can breathe. In this sense, it has always been a place of grace for me.

I think of the number of times I have been surprised by grace while walking on Carmel Beach. One day in particular while looking out at the ocean, I witnessed not one, but two gorgeous rainbows. The colors were vivid and alive, stretching from one end of the bay to another. I had no plans to see a double rainbow over the ocean that day, nor did my travel agent arrange it. It came to me as pure gift and, therefore, pure joy.

Another day whales swam so close to the shore that I could literally see the markings on the skin of those majestic creatures. They were playing and frolicking in the water, just being whales of course; but to me they brought a moment of pure and utter grace.

On still another day, I watched for nearly an hour as dolphins leapt from the water, gracefully swimming in the waves and sunlight. They would thread their way in and out of the waves with such grace that it was nothing less than inspiring. Again, it was a gift.

I didn't do one thing to earn these moments. Certainly nothing inside of me was worthy of them. Grace happens! Of all the times of the year when we need to find grace, surely the Christmas season is one of the most important. This is why I would encourage you to let go of some of your trying. Not all of it, of course. There's a place for trying harder, for planning and preparing and making good things happen for yourself and family. But there is also a place for not trying, for relaxing and letting go, a time to open the heart and allow God to surprise you in the midst of a demanding holiday season. Sometimes trying harder is the very winter from which we need respite. It's all right to give yourself a break. It's all right to exhale and let down. It's only when we are able to let go that something surprising, something graceful, can flow toward us.

Think about it like this: We can work and hone certain skills in life, but in the end, all that work has to be released so that something remarkable can happen. The actor may work long hours perfecting the part and memorizing the lines, but when she walks on the stage to deliver them, she has to release the tension from her voice and body, relax and let the performance happen. Otherwise the genius of the writing and the energy of the performance will not flow to the audience.

Christmas is the season to relax with our faith, to let go of trying harder, trying to please, and trying to be all things to all people. Something is drawing near to us, something beautiful and poetic. That something is nothing less than God's presence and grace. When Jesus was born in Bethlehem, he was nothing more than a helpless, quivering, sweet, tremulous, lovely little boy. That's it, just the miracle of a baby. God's approach was not, "Here are my expectations found in this manual. If you meet them, then I will love you." Nor did God say, "Here are the defining beliefs for being a Christian. If you can subscribe to them, then I will accept you." None of that was at the beginning of the Christian story.

Instead, it was only that vulnerable baby, his tiny fingers moving in the air, his eyes barely open, his mouth making sweet sucking sounds on Mary's breast. He was God's poetry and grace, surely as mystical and wonderful as a double rainbow over Carmel Bay, a whale swimming in the sea, or the flashing body of a dolphin leaping from the water.

We are coming closer and closer to Christmas.

Is Christmas coming closer and closer to you?

O God of grace, I have been trying hard my entire life. Trying to please others. Trying to make a good impression. Trying to succeed. In so many ways, my trying has gotten in the way of my living. Even as I move closer and closer to the celebration of Christmas morning, may the true grace of Christmas touch my life again. I am ready to be surprised. Amen.

DECEMBER 18

Paying Attention to Our Dreams

And having been warned in a dream not to return to Herod,
they left for their own country by another road.

MATTHEW 2:12

One theme woven into the story of the Christ child is dreams. I'm not talking about the dreams we have concerning our goals and aspirations in life. Those are certainly important. I am thinking about those nighttime visitations associated with the Spirit. You might even think of them as wisdom from the soul. Dreams are composed of symbols, images, and inner characters. They draw near to us when we close our eyes and allow our conscious minds to rest.

In the Christmas story, a dream encourages Joseph to love Mary and keep her as his wife. A dream warns him to flee to Egypt to protect the Christ child from harm. Even the magi follow a dream and leave the child without returning to Herod. Beyond the birth story, dreams play an important role in many biblical stories, perhaps most famously in the book of Genesis with the stories about Jacob and Joseph.

For several years I did a significant amount of dream work with a Jungian therapist. I still take time to write my dreams in a journal. If you want to become serious about listening to your dreams, you might consider consulting a therapist or spiritual director. I believe in the power of dreams to speak to our lives. Even if you choose not to work with your dreams, you can still begin to listen and learn from them. In some instances, you may even sense the direction God is trying to lead you. I often tell people, even if you don't "interpret" your dreams, just taking time to reflect on them is a good spiritual practice.

A couple of thoughts about working with your dreams...

One assumption in dream work is that the language of dreams is almost always symbolic. Sometimes the content of their dreams bothers people. They slough them off as "weird" or "crazy" or "odd." Don't take your dreams literally. Dreams use the language of symbolism, symbols that are cross-culturally important to both religion and psychology. A simple example is the symbol of water. A multifaceted symbol, water can be a sign of chaos or an experience of undifferentiated feeling and thought. Water can also be a symbol of purity and rebirth. Before we can have rebirth, we must first plunge into dark, undifferentiated waters. To begin listening to dreams requires us to pay attention to symbolic language, asking the question of meaning and significance at a new level of depth.

This symbolism also applies to people who appear in our dreams. For example, when I dream about my daughter, it's not really about my daughter. It's about some dimension in me that my daughter represents. I often have dreams about my mother, especially since she passed away a few years ago; but the dream is not literally about my mother. It's about something in me represented by the figure of my mother. Therefore dreams, much like biblical texts, have to be listened to below the surface. Understanding our dreams is important if we are going to listen to our soul. This is one of the most crucial dimensions in our spiritual life, not rushing to find an answer, but sitting still with our deepest emotions and inner symbols.

In this way, dreams become a kind of language of the soul. One way to think about it is this: Our conscious mind is so busy, stressed and running 100 m.p.h., that it's hard for the soul to speak. (Maybe I should say "hard for *God* to speak"?) When the conscious mind finally relaxes, it allows another door to open. That door is the deeper world of soul. I don't think of dreams as objects we are trying to interpret (as if we are trying to read an esoteric roadmap) as much as I think of them as the opportunity to listen to the softer voices of our being.

To listen to our depths is important, especially when we are experiencing a personal winter. In fact, sometimes our souls thrust us into a kind of winter so that we might finally begin to do the listening we have ignored in our spiritual lives. (I might also add that this is why prayer is so important, why finding time for quiet meditation or sharing in the eucharist on a regular basis is important.) We close the door of the conscious mind for a few moments, and we open ourselves to the transforming presence of images, characters, and spiritual figures. What we don't hear at the conscious level makes its way to us through the unconscious dimension of our dreams.

I believe the metaphor of listening is not only appropriate for our dreams; it is the central image of the spiritual life. When we begin listening to our dreams, we engage our imagination; and imagination is critical to our faith. It's sometimes helpful to be playful in our listening, particularly with dreams that come to us like angels in the night. Many times what we need in life is not a "cure" or "fix" for our problems. What we need are images that break open something new and fresh, something that engages our imagination.

An example might be the image of darkness. Thanks to writers such as Carl Jung and Thomas Moore, I have come to appreciate the image of darkness in a new way. Darkness, especially in Christian theology, is often viewed as the enemy that must be defeated. Yet what if that image can be imagined differently? What if darkness can become a gift? What if genuine life can emerge from our darkness? And in reality it does! From the darkness of the womb comes the life of a child.

In much the same way, dreams give us images that spark the imagination. Rather than seeing the images as peculiar objects of passing fancy, I more and more think of them as playful opportunities to imagine my life differently. What does it mean that I had a dream of a great house? What does it mean that I had a dream of a church with a jade green center aisle? What does it mean that a horse appears again and again in my dreams? To listen to our dreams means we listen and ponder certain images; it's another way of paying attention to God.

Listen to the stories of scripture. Listen to the traditions of the church. Listen to your deepest feelings. But also listen this day to the language of the soul, to the angels that come to us again and again in our dreams. They may not automatically lead us out of our winter, but surely they will keep us company. As Mary and Joseph discovered, sometimes they bring us to memorable new beginnings. How amazing it is to know and feel that whether waking or sleeping, God is at work in our world and always drawing near to our lives.

Help me, O God, to listen to you in every way possible. Especially in the upcoming quiet season after the holidays, help me to listen to my dreams. May the right image, the right insight, the right awareness be discovered in all my listening. Forgive me when I am so hurried and busy that I fail to grasp (and be grasped by) your spiritual truths. In this season when I linger with memories of Christmas and hopes for a new year, I want to become a better listener to your voice. Amen.

DECEMBER 19

Praising God in the Midst of Living

Jesus answered, "I am the way, and the truth, and the life."

JOHN 14:6a

Every now and then a poem not only speaks to me, but the timing of receiving it creates new layers of meaning for the work of art itself. This was especially true when I first discovered a poem by Adam Zagajewski entitled "Try to Praise the Mutilated World."[13] My oldest son sent the poem to me. The day I received it, I had to conduct a funeral for a young man in my congregation who had taken his own life. His family was living through a nightmarish winter. Hurt, angry, and sad, they were asking questions that will never be answered.

All people suffer. In our suffering we look for God's comfort. But tragedy is different. It sometimes leaves us too numb to search for answers, and too disoriented to ask the questions that might eventually help us. We see tragedy in the world as we watch the news night after

---

[13]In Adam Zagajewski, *Without End: New and Selected Poems* (New York: Farrar, Straus and Giroux, 2002), 60.

night; but when it happens to people we know and love, people we have shared a life with inside a family or congregation, then the suffering can almost turn our hearts to stone. On the day of this young man's service, I didn't know how or what I might say that could bring comfort to his family. I didn't want to use clichés or offer a string of religious bromides. At the same time, something needed to be said, something of hope and help for this grieving family, as well as a final word of dignity for the young man.

The poem arrived via e-mail early on the morning of the service. This lovely, beautifully written poem provided hope for me that day in the midst of a world gone wrong. It might bring hope to you. The poet never uses the words *faith* or *God* or *Christ*; nevertheless it's a profoundly religious poem. It reminds the reader that it requires enormous faith to affirm life in the midst of a broken world. This surely goes to the heart of the Christmas message, a message of life in the midst of so much brokenness.

Try to Praise the Mutilated World

Try to praise the mutilated world.
Remember June's long days,
and wild strawberries, drops of rose wine.
The nettles that methodically overgrow
the abandoned homesteads of exiles.
You must praise the mutilated world.
You watched the stylish yachts and ships;
one of them had a long trip ahead of it,
while salty oblivion awaited others.
You've seen the refugees going nowhere,
you've heard the executioners sing joyfully.
You should praise the mutilated world.
Remember the moments when we were together
in a white room and the curtain fluttered.
Return in thought to the concert where music flared.
You gathered acorns in the park in autumn

and leaves eddied over the earth's scars.
Praise the mutilated world
and the gray feather a thrush lost,
and the gentle light that strays and vanishes
and returns.

The poem has a kind of urgency to which I'm drawn, an insistence that life requires courage for us to be faithful. The poet leaves no room for wavering (as if we could otherwise) and boldly states: *You must praise the mutilated world.* Why? Well, because the mutilated world is all we have. Perhaps it will be all we'll ever have. If we're waiting on the world to improve before we discover joy, experience peace, or engage love, then we'll be waiting a long time. Just as trying harder isn't always the answer to our lives of faith, nor is waiting for things to get better an answer either.

I'm always amazed when December rolls around. It seems as if something is happening every year that makes Christmas not merely nice for our family celebrations but absolutely necessary for the survival of our humanity. Think for a moment that Christ is not so much the person of Jesus, but is creative, transforming, spiritual energy. Christmas was an instance of Christ energy coalescing in the life of Jesus of Nazareth, but doesn't Christ energy come together in remarkable ways again and again?

To experience Christ, therefore, does not mean we sit around thinking about the person whom we call Jesus Christ. (Though there is certainly a time and place for that.) Christ energy pulses through the world. To follow Zagajewski's lead, it can be found in the luscious strawberry, in the long June afternoon, in making love to another human being, in a concert of exquisite music, even in the lost feather of a thrush.

Christ energy is all around us. Therefore, not only *can* we praise the mutilated world, we *must* praise it. But before we can praise it, we have to pay attention to it. That is precisely what Christmas invites us to do—to wake up and pay attention to the world today. Not waiting on it to get better or rearrange itself. Not even waiting on ourselves to become better. But to take today as it is right now, observing the beauty of each moment, beauty like the baby Jesus himself, and therefore embracing these moments as signs of Christ's energy in the world.

Such a viewpoint is not necessarily an easy one to believe and practice. The mutilated world can be overwhelming. But some days praising the mutilated world is all we can do. I don't remember much of what I said to that grieving family in my eulogy that day. I just remember that I received an e-mail poem from my son. I read it that morning and treasure it to this day. I also remember that I made a copy and sent it to the family a few days later.

I wasn't sure if I should do that or not.

But I did.

They told me they liked it.

O God, I pray for every person in the world today who is experiencing a dark, cold winter. Forgive me when I don't quite know what to do or say to help others. But in the midst of every winter, I pray that you will give me the capacity to discover Christ. Not just Christ as a person of history. Not just Christ the subject of doctrines and beliefs. But Christ as redemptive love, as creative hope, as loving relationship. Amen.

DECEMBER 20

Grace Touches Us All

On entering the house, they saw the child with Mary his mother; and they knelt down and paid him homage. Then, opening their treasure chests, they offered him gifts of gold, frankincense, and myrrh.

MATTHEW 2:11

For some reason, I associate Isak Dinesen's "Babette's Feast" with the holiday season. It's not a Christmas story, but the story of a young woman exiled from Paris who winds up in a small, extremely strict religious community in France. The two sisters in charge of the community have pity on the young woman, graciously feed her, and give her safety. Babette regains her strength and remains with the community because she has no other good alternative. A famous chef in Paris before her exile, she ends up doing all of the cooking.

Unfortunately, the people in the community were so narrow in their appreciation of life that they never really enjoyed food. They ate the same thing day after day. Food nourished their bodies, but they never associated taste and pleasure with this common activity. Their kind of asceticism required them to follow meticulously the rules of the community and to practice self-denial. Never under any circumstances were they to delight in such things.

As the story unfolds, Babette learns she's been awarded a large sum of money. She could use the money to fund her return to Paris so she could begin her life again. But something has happened to her while sharing in this community of faith. She is enormously grateful for their goodness toward her; after all, they saved her life. In gratitude, she decides to take all of the money, buy food, and prepare a feast for everyone in the community. She shops for several days, buying everything from turtles to pigeons, wine, bread, and exotic spices. It takes her almost a week to prepare the extravagant feast.

Finally, the night comes to share in the meal. Everyone in the religious community, as well as a few friends, gather around the exquisitely set table. Each of them has decided beforehand not to enjoy the meal. They will taste it and be courteous to Babette because they have come to love her.

The meal is served in multiple courses, each course becoming more complex, beautiful, and luscious. As the elaborate dinner progresses from course to course, the taste, smells, and presentation of the food begin to transform them. They become aware of how much love has been poured into the food. More importantly they realize Babette has abandoned herself into the preparation of this amazing feast. In spite of their conspiracy not to enjoy the meal, it has become a spectacle of love and generosity.

They also witness something else, perhaps for the first time in their lives. They see that all of God's creation, including the food on their table, is good. They learn it's not sinful to experience pleasure and that this feeling doesn't lead them away from God at all. On the contrary, it can bring them closer to the Divine. Although it's clear they are enjoying every decadent bite, no one dares utter a single word of appreciation.

Eventually the elegance of the dinner so spiritually moves one dinner guest, a longtime friend of the community, that he rises and says to everyone around the table,

"We have all of us been told that grace is to be found in the universe. But in our human foolishness and shortsightedness we imagine divine grace to be finite...but the moment comes when our eyes are opened and we see and realize that grace is infinite. Grace, my friends, demands nothing from us but that we shall await it with confidence and acknowledge it in gratitude...Grace takes us to its bosom and proclaims general amnesty...I have learned tonight that anything is possible."[14]

To believe that grace is infinite is to understand the essence of Christmas. For so many of us, we live in a perpetual winter because we do not trust that there is enough—not enough love, not enough grace, not enough goodness. Sometimes we become desperate, working and straining at life in such a way that nothing good can draw near because we're just not open enough to receive it. Life changes when we begin to believe that grace is infinite. Then we can await it with confidence. Surely Christmas invites us to believe this truth, to trust it even in the bleakest of winters.

Something utterly extravagant marked the first Christmas. Angels are singing, shepherds are inspired, Magi begin their journey, and a star appears in the sky. This extravagance is a sign of how God works in the world, drawing close to us with ample grace and love, and, of course, setting a large enough table for all people. We give gifts to one another on Christmas morning to honor the central truth that God's love has been given to us as a gift in Christ. Therefore, if Christmas is grace, then the only right and proper response we can make toward it is gratitude.

That's why Babette prepared her feast for her adopted community. It's also why we offer our own gifts to the world. We don't have to worry about whether they are great or small. In some ways, we don't even have to worry if our gifts are well received by others. We don't give for approval or recognition or to receive something in return.

---

[14]Isak Dinesen, "Babette's Feast," in *Anecdotes of Destiny and Ehrengard* (New York: Vintage Books, 1993), 54.

Instead, we practice kindness and compassion, extend love, and offer ourselves in service to others. We also practice forgiveness and gentleness because we are responding to the largest of God's infinite grace given to us in the Christ child.

As we near the joy of Christmas day, I would encourage you to reflect in two different ways. First of all, consider what grace is coming close to you. What gifts are being presented to your life right now? And secondly, consider how you might impart grace to another person. Why not give a gift of complete extravagance to someone? To receive with the right hand and give with the left hand is the natural spiritual rhythm of life. Enjoy it! Live it!

O God of all extravagance, each day you set a table upon which you invite me to feast. Friends and family. The beauty of each day. For the many ways you draw near to me, gracious God, I am thankful. I simply ask for the inspiration to live with a grateful heart, giving myself to others and inviting others unto myself. Amen.

DECEMBER 21

Eternal Music, Eternal Dance

Then shall the young women rejoice in the dance,
*   and the young men and the old shall be merry.*
*   I will turn their mourning into joy, I will comfort them,*
and give them gladness for sorrow.

JEREMIAH 31:13

Picture a seventeen-year-old-girl. Terry works on a ranch in Idaho, nature's beauty surrounding her in stunning fashion—majestic mountains, magnificent streams teeming with rainbow trout, and a marvelous azure blue sky. This young woman is searching, searching for herself perhaps, but she is also on a spiritual search for God.

One night alone in her cabin praying, a kind of vision suddenly appears. A figure draped in a white robe of light stands at the foot of her bed. Was it a dream? Was it a literal vision? Was it her imagination? I don't really know, nor does she. All I know is that she was searching for something in her life, and it appeared, then disappeared.

She started to shake and felt a burning sensation inside her body. Then she did the only thing she knew to do. She called her mother, who lived six hours away in Salt Lake City. When she awoke for breakfast the next morning, a simple message was waiting for her from her mother and grandmother, "Kathryn and I are on our way up. Love you. Mom."

Terry Tempest Williams grew up to be a marvelous writer, naturalist, and tireless advocate for the environment. A deep, spiritual awareness runs throughout all her writing. Listen to how she describes this unsettling adolescent moment.

I was leaning against the buck n'rail fence waiting for them. When I saw both of them coming down the dirt road, I began to cry. They both held me and one of them said, "Let's go."

We drove to Mesa Falls on a narrow, winding road through the lodgepole forest, parked the car and walked to the overlook. The force and volume of the cascading water articulated my own spiritual free fall…The three of us watched in silence; a rainbow arched over the falls. I told them my story all over again.

I told them that "I knelt down by the side of my bed and told my Heavenly Father that I had sincerely read and studied the scriptures, that I had a deep desire to know if the Church was true…(And then) a small, narrow figure, surrounded by light, as though it was being seen from a great distance, stood at the foot of my bed. It was…"

"What dear?" my mother asked.

"It was—I don't know—I don't know if I was seeing things or it if was real. Something moved through my body like a current. Heat, warmth, I can't describe it. And then the figure disappeared."

And then as a young woman of seventeen years still unable to trust what I had just shared, I asked the women in my life who mattered most if they believed me, if they thought this apparition meant the Church was true.

"Nobody can answer that for you. The question isn't really whether or not the Church is true," my grandmother Mimi said, pausing. "It's all true," my grandmother said, looking out at the great expanse before us. "All of this is true."[15]

On this first official day of winter, the shortest day and longest night of the year, is it really true? Is God always with us?

So many times we think we have to be good enough for God because if we are not, then God might not be with us. Or we think we have to know the Bible well enough because if we don't, we might inadvertently get it all wrong and not find God. Or we think we have to act a certain way because if we don't, God might reject us. What does it mean to believe God is always with us?

Maybe God is like *music*. God is not a phantom figure moving in and out of history (sometimes present, sometimes absent). God is like music that touches the soul. Have you noticed how you can hear music without really hearing it? I can listen to a choir during church or go to a concert in a recital hall. When the last note has sounded, the music plays on inside my soul. Sometimes the literal music I hear with my ears triggers a kind of inner music inside my heart. God is with us like music. Like the soundtrack of a movie that supports the unfolding plot and characters of the film, God's music supports everything we are and hope to be. Similar to Terry Tempest Williams, we may have certain moments that vividly remind us of God's presence; but the reminder is simply this: whether we hear the literal music of God or not, divine music is, in fact, playing through us all the time.

Maybe God is like *dance*. God is an endless choreography forever moving inside our lives. To observe dance is to see beauty, true poetry in motion. Dance is the human body stretched upon a canvas of air. Dance honors space and closeness, the expected and unexpected. But what happens when we see dance? When we see it, really see it, it begins to release the dance present within us. We feel the loveliness of it, the movement, the aching beauty and wondrous energy. Something *external* touches something deeply *internal*. Without words, we eventually

---

[15]Terry Tempest Williams, *Leap* (New York: Pantheon, 2000), 28.

find what is *eternal*, namely the divine Word. We may not be dancing ourselves, but witnessing dance releases a kind of poetry within us.

I love Gwendolyn Brooks's poetry because she captured the African American experience on the south side of Chicago, where she lived her entire life. You can read her poetry and feel the glory and tragedy of urban life: all the sights, sounds, and smells of the city. After she won the Pulitzer Prize in 1950, she explained, "I write about what I see and hear in the street. I live in a small second-floor apartment at the corner, and I look first on one side and then the other. There is my material."[16]

Where is God? Is God always with us? These are the winter questions we ask from time to time. But all we have to do is look out the window of our lives. There we'll find the material! Advent is not so much about our celebrating the coming of God into the world, as it is our opening up to the presence that is radically incarnated into all of life. That is the real truth of Christmas. We are given a privilege today, the first day of winter, to hear the music and see the dance, thus experiencing the divine presence that is with us at all times. Christmas reminds us, as a grandmother remarked to her seventeen-year-old granddaughter in front of a waterfall: "This is true. All of it!" That might even be said about our deepest, darkest winters.

O singing God and dancing God, help me to hear the beauty of your music and follow the choreography of your Spirit each day. And most of all, help me to discover the truth of your presence in all times and places, to know that you are near, to know that you are real, to know that you are love. Amen.

---

[16]Mel Watkins, "Gwendolyn Brooks, 83, Passionate Poet, Dies," *The New York Times*, 5 December 2000, 22.

DECEMBER 22

The Adventure of Growing

> *...work out your own salvation with fear and trembling; for it is God who is at work in you, enabling you both to will and to work for his good pleasure.*

PHILIPPIANS 2:12B–13

In *Finding Your Religion*, Scotty McLennan, dean of religious life at Stanford University, explores stages of religious development. Just as we develop physically, emotionally, and intellectually as human beings, McLennan argues that we also go through stages of religious development.[17] This concept of an evolving faith is an interesting one, especially during a season when religious reflection is heightened.

He calls the first stage the *Magic Stage*. During this stage of development, God is all-powerful. Spiritual life is a stage of demons and fairies, ghosts and spiritual dragons. Perhaps this is the most childish stage of faith. In a certain way, the celebration of Christmas

---

[17]All references to the stages of religious development found in this essay are from Scotty McLennan, *Finding Your Religion* (San Francisco: HarperSanFrancisco, 1999).

appeals to our sense of magic—angels and stars, and, of course, the magi.

The second stage is the *Reality Stage*. I see many Christians who seem to be stuck in the reality stage. God is seen as the cause and effect of everything in the world. The Bible is taken as a literal book of truth. People believe they can influence God by trying to be good: "If I will just do this or that, God will be with me and protect me."

The third stage McLennan identifies as the *Dependence Stage*. During this stage, God is the authority figure, usually a parent and typically a father. Some of us want a dependent relationship with God because we didn't enjoy a healthy relationship with our parents. Therefore, if we don't experience this with God, we oftentimes turn a human religious leader into an authority figure.

The fourth stage is the *Independence Stage*. In this stage, God is viewed as a more distant reality. No longer the personal buddy, God becomes a transcending force in human experience. During this stage we begin to see our spiritual lives as unique. We become uncomfortable with the idea that all Christians have to look alike, think alike, and worship alike. We start de-emphasizing the personal dimension of God and begin appreciating God as ultimate reality.

The *Interdependent Stage* is a time in life when we start synthesizing our faith. Instead of seeing God as completely separate, we begin to see God as near and far, close and distant. We become comfortable with paradox. We see our faith as unique, but we also feel our need to be part of a faith community. God can be seen as energy and ultimate reality, just as images of shepherd, mother, or father can be used to enhance faith. Faith can also be both answer and question!

The final stage McLennan mentions is the *Unity Stage*. In this stage God is all-pervasive. All religious traditions begin to have value and wisdom. We might even cross over to find new insights from other religious pathways. This is why near the end of his life Thomas Merton said that the more he became Christian the more he became Jewish, the more he became Jewish the more he became Buddhist, the more he became Buddhist the more he became Catholic. He wasn't giving up his Christian faith. On the contrary, it was leading him to greater and greater religious consciousness.

McLennan's stages raise some important questions during this season of religious celebration: Is your religious consciousness evolving? Are you stuck in a dependency stage? Are you stuck in the independence stage and now need to move to a greater synthesis of faith? Is it time to experience interdependence with your faith? Could you be growing toward the edges of a unity stage? One thing is for sure. Rarely is the religious journey a straight line. True faith is always changing; yet that's when faith becomes exciting because *becoming* is what it's all about.

Moving from one stage to another can begin to feel like a spiritual winter. One way of thinking or believing might work for a while, but then we find ourselves transitioning to something else. What happens most often is that we are ready to leave something behind before we know what it is we are going to embrace. This experience of not knowing can feel desolate. Part of faith means that we risk such a season because we sense something worth discovering on the other side.

From virtually every perspective, the Christmas story is characterized by a series of unknowns. Mary didn't know what would happen to her after the annunciation of her pregnancy. Joseph did not know what to do with Mary, and the shepherds didn't know exactly why they were praising God. The magi did not know what they would find as they traveled toward the child, nor did King Herod know what kind of king Jesus would eventually become. Yet in the midst of so many unknowns, people listened and learned. In some cases, they were radically transformed.

One of the gifts of Christmas is that it extends God's invitation for us to grow and deepen our humanity. Salvation comes to us as a gift with pure love and grace, but it also empowers us to move through our many stages of faith. Or, in the words of the apostle Paul, we "work out [our] salvation with fear and trembling" (Phil. 2:12). We are free to explore and ask questions, free to challenge our faith even as our faith challenges us. It is sad when people turn Christianity into an "answer book" faith. At the same time, it's just as sad when people have the freedom to grow in their faith, but neglect doing so because of misplaced priorities or simply because they are apathetic toward the spiritual life.

The point of Christmas is not to reach one day of celebration and then put it all behind us. Christmas is trying to reach us! The manifestation of God's love in the Christ child offers us an adventure of living and growing. Something is trying to ripen within us, and the ripening of our lives goes through many stages and seasons. Regardless of where you find yourself this Christmas season, use it as an opportunity to move forward (even into the unknown) and trust that the call to grow is always a call from God.

Loving God, you make yourself known in so many different ways. I give thanks for your presence in Jesus Christ. May something of the beauty and mystery of Christmas reach me. Help me to move forward, to deepen my humanity, to stretch my understanding of faith. In the many stages of life experience, let me always rest assured of the one reality that never changes—your unconditional love. Amen.

The Winter's Holy Days

SECTION FOUR

DECEMBER 23

Opting for Hope

May the God of hope fill you with all joy and peace in believing, so that you may abound in hope by the power of the Holy Spirit.

ROMANS 15:13

For the past few years, I've gone through a period of questioning regarding my faith in God. That's not an easy admission for a minister, but it's true. I have questioned everything essential about my religion: Is there really a God? What language best serves my religious faith? Who was Jesus? What does Jesus mean for the world today? What does it mean to even confess Christ as Lord and Savior? What is the role of religious faith in the world, particularly at a time when religion seems so damaging and divisive to the human family?

It's not often that a minister expresses these doubts (let alone talks about them publicly). To do so runs the risk of hurting the faith of other people, and that's the last thing any minister wants to do. Yet much to my surprise, anytime I have shared my questions and doubts with others, rather than hurting them, it actually serves to strengthen heir spiritual journeys. Sometimes it even gives them permission to rticulate their own questions. Many times, these thoughts have been ilently smuggled through a lifetime of attending Sunday school classes nd church services.

When you have doubts, you are forced to ask yourself, "What do I really believe about life?" What you once believed is not necessarily what you believe now, nor does it mean that you will believe it in the future. Sometimes our beliefs can't keep up with our experiences in life; therefore, we have doubts about what we believe. This is why a simple theological "gut-check" on where you're at in any given moment can be a positive exercise.

Several years ago a reporter asked Oprah Winfrey, "What are you are certain about now?" Surprised by the question, she was slightly embarrassed that she didn't really have an answer. She went home and began some inner reflection, forcing herself to answer the question about what she believed to be true about life.

During any spiritual winter, the leaves of what we have believed might be stripped and blown away, but the tree remains, as do the branches and roots. It's good to ask from time to time: "What do *I* most believe about life?" Christmas is as good a time as any to ask such a question, because Christmas brings us home to what we most believe about ourselves and the universe.

One way I would summarize my answer of certainty would be this: *I believe in living with the power of hope.* Even if some of my cherished beliefs may be wrong, even if I might be off base on *this* theological issue or *that* doctrine of the church, in the end, I believe in living with hope. Even if I am disappointed with life, even if tragedy strikes or disappointment comes, I believe in living with hope. Hope is not necessarily the same as optimism. Nor is it living naively with rose-colored glasses. Evil and heartache are real, but evil and heartache do not have to be the defining reality of my experience.

A few years ago, Father Andrew Greeley wrote a deeply personal expression about his own journey of faith, about a time when he, too, was searching and questioning his place in the universe. He concluded that we really have only two choices in life. One goes along the lines o Shakespeare's *Macbeth,* who contended that, "[Life] is a tale / Told by an idiot, full of sound and fury, / Signifying nothing."[18] Or a person could go the other direction and follow philosopher Teilhard de Chardin's statement, "Something is afoot in the universe, something that looks like gestation and birth."

Greeley decided that we can either live with a sense of plan and purpose, believing that who we are and what we do really matters or we can choose to live in a cruel, arbitrary, deceptive cosmos in which who we are has no lasting consequence. Interestingly enough, Greeley acknowledges that the data is "inconclusive." That's important to note. Sometimes people of faith overstate their experience to the point that it undermines the very thing they are trying to affirm. Is it possible that we live in an arbitrary universe? Is it possible that we are only a speck of dust and that when life is over, it's over and that's it? I suppose the answer is yes, it is possible. Father Greeley, however, concludes his thoughts in a way that makes perfect sense to me. He says the he opts for hope, not as an irrational choice in the face of the facts, but as a leap of faith in the goodness he has experienced.

On the brink of another Christmas holiday, I hope you can affirm what is true, at least in my experience: Time and time again, I have participated in the goodness of life. I have been the recipient of love and have been forgiven and accepted by friends. I know what it's like to walk beside the ocean and feel at one with the universe. I have been moved to tears by the beauty of art, books, and poetry. I have fallen, and in ways I don't understand, been able to stand up and live again. In spite of the bleakness of the world (and there is plenty of it), I have seen gesture after gesture of charity and kindness, compassion and generosity. I have no doubt or question about these things, only amazement and gratitude.

Maybe this is why I love Christmas so much. I don't need to argue and prove theories about the virgin birth. I have no need to debate

---

[18]*Macbeth,* 5.5.29–31.

whether or not Jesus was actually born in the city of Bethlehem or some other town. I do not have to decide what elements of the birth narratives are historically true and which are theological symbols. Christmas gave hope to the world because people came to believe God was doing a profound thing, some new thing in the life of this child. Christmas still gives hope to the world because it invites us to believe again that something good and beautiful is still released into the universe through the life of Jesus. This means that no matter how hapless the world, it's never hopeless.

Christmas is the perfect time to affirm with my colleague Andrew Greeley: I opt for hope! Is there a way for you to live with hope? Is there a way for you to reaffirm life's goodness? To do so will not only make for a better Christmas; it will make for a better life.

O God, give me the courage to live with hope, not only for myself, but for my family and church and world. Forgive my many questions, and overlook my incessant doubts. In all things, however, help me to move forward into life, believing that you call all of your children into the future with hope and love. Thank you for Christmas and the many good memories I have of it. Amen.

DECEMBER 24

The Pause between the Notes

But the angel said to them, "Do not be afraid; for see—I am bringing you good news of great joy for all the people: to you is born this day in the city of David a Savior, who is the Messiah, the Lord.

LUKE 2:10–11

When I think about the first Christmas, I think of it as an event shrouded in silence. Perhaps that comes from too many years of singing "Silent Night, Holy Night" on Christmas Eve with the sanctuary darkened and candles uplifted by the congregation.

Can you begin to imagine that night, that silent night of his birth? Mary and Joseph are traveling. He is very quiet, worrying about where they will spend the night. Mary's ankles are swollen, her belly heavy with child. Truth be told, she doesn't feel like talking much to anyone. The birth happens in a barn—dark, quiet, and cavernous. A cow bellows every once in a while. Occasionally, a horse offers a wet, mucousy snort. Or you might even hear a diminutive mouse rustle in the hay. It was a quiet, silent night when he was born.

I see Mary's eyes becoming large—dark like the eyes of a pony. They are dilated with adrenaline, and she is breathing hard, eventually panting and pushing. For the first time in their relationship, Joseph sees and hears her weep. He thinks she is beautiful, even while weeping. Then comes that brief sound of suction, of life coming out of the hollow of her body, and yes, a baby squiggling into the world for the first time. A tender slap is administered to his skin. Then Jesus (at this moment a baby like any other baby) sucks down the sweetness of oxygen. He is wrapped in cotton towels and gently placed upon the chest of his mother. She breathes. The baby breathes. And then more silence.

A little poem from the fifteenth century goes like this:

> Lo, in the silent night
> A child to God is born
> And all is brought again
> That ere was lost or lorn.
> Could but thy soul, O man,
> Become a silent night!
> God would be born in thee
> And set all things aright.[19]

We can look at Christmas in two ways. One way is to focus on what happened to Jesus. We should think about Jesus on Christmas Eve and about how in the life of this child God brought a message of healing and hope to the world. The curtain was pulled back, and the essence of God was revealed: a God willing to empty God's self to participate in the human experience, to love human beings to the point of God's own suffering. When we look back on the first Christmas, we see it as a proclamation of God's peace upon the entire creation, God's hope that there will be goodwill toward all creatures, God's highest desire to be reconciled to the human family. Christmas reminds us of the mystery of Jesus—that he embodied divine life, that he is the Son

---

[19]Author unknown, "Lo, In the Silent Night," *in Watch for the Light: Readings for Advent and Christmas* (Farmington, Pa.: Plough Publishing House, 2001), 1.

of God, yet deeply human, reminding us that God works through flesh, blood, and bone. We need the baby who was quietly born in Bethlehem centuries ago.

We can focus on Christmas in another way. In some ways, it's even more important than the first. We can focus on the possibility that Christ could be born in us, that his spirit could reshape our spirits, that his compassion could be sculpted into our personalities, and that his love and courage could be incarnated within our flesh. In some ways, having Christ born in Bethlehem was the easy part; having Christ born within *us*, within a twenty-first–century world, is much more challenging. But it is possible. It's still possible for you and for me, but only if we make room for him to be born, only possible when we learn to listen to our silent nights.

That is why I love the silence of Christmas Eve. It speaks to us. Only when a space has been cleared or a pause has been created can we become quiet enough for Christ to be born within us. Some of us want noise all the time. We want things all the time. We want clutter, success, and good health all the time. We want to be entertained all the time. We want achievement all the time. But spiritual transformation only happens when we pause to listen to the deepest voice of all, the voice of God within each of us. What does God say to you today? Not in a literal voice, not in a voice from above, but from within, from the depths of your being, what does God say to you on this Christmas Eve?

I hope you will hear the voice that says, "You are loved, and you have a place in the world." Listen for the voice that says, "I believe in you. I still have a purpose for you, regardless of how long your winter has become." Heed the voice that says, "You are capable of good things, maybe even great things in life; and if you are ready to start, I will help you." Be ready for the voice that says, "No matter what happens to you, I will be with you and never leave you." Don't miss the voice that says, "I will give you the courage you need to live your one, wild, precious life!"

What does God say to you this Christmas Eve?

The poet Theodore Roethke once said, "In a dark time, the eye begins to see."[20] It's also true that in a silent night, the ear begins to hear. What does God say to you this holy night? Christmas may have started in silence, but it was not all silence. In that one holy birth, God spoke to the world. Love and hope had arrived. God still speaks on Christmas Eve and invites us to live again, to move past old hurts and step out with courage. The angels split the heavens as their song etched its way along a night sky that first Christmas. The shepherds rejoiced, and the magi traveled with gifts. Yes, it started in silence; but it ended in song because grace had arrived.

If we will just listen to the silence—listen and listen and listen—grace will still arrive. I encourage you to pause between the notes of busyness and celebration to listen. What will be born inside your soul this day? Unlike other days during the year when silence might be uncomfortable if not oppressive, the silence of this day speaks. It speaks if we will listen. *Because if "thy soul [could] / Become a silent night… / God would be born in thee / And set all things aright."*

In the silence of this Christmas Eve, I listen, O God. I listen for your voice of love, your presence of hope, your inspiration of joy. Let me know again the joy of my salvation. I pray for the world today. I pray that every restless heart will find a moment of peace. With Christians around the world, I bow and give thanks once again for your love given to me in Christ. Amen.

[20]Theodore Roethke, *The Collected Poems of Theodore Roethke* (New York: Anchor Press/Doubleday, 1975), 231.

DECEMBER 25

Christ Is Born This Day!

...until she had borne a son; and he named him Jesus.

MATTHEW 1:25B

With each passing year, I recognize that Christmas is celebrated in many different ways and with many different moods. I'm not talking about cultural differences and customs; instead, I'm thinking of the psychological air created and breathed by people on Christmas Day. What are you feeling today? What are the realities of your Christmas?

If you are part of a young family, Christmas means gifts and chaotic bedlam around the tree: happily unwrapping presents, assembling toys, and making a last-minute trip to the drugstore to buy forgotten AAA batteries. Maybe you are traveling today, trying to visit both sets of grandparents and not wanting to favor one side of the family over the other. That's stress! Perhaps you live alone but will spend the day with friends and neighbors. For days now you've been planning a delicious meal and have purchased a special gift for each guest. Some of you are alone today, and it feels just fine. There's nothing wrong with being alone, including being alone on Christmas. But maybe it's not all right.

Maybe we'll remember different times, better times when life was richer and fuller. One thing is for sure: Rarely is Christmas Day a perfect one.

I learned this lesson early in my life. I will never forget one particular Christmas Day. I'm guessing I was about ten years old. My great-grandmother, Edith, had been ill and hospitalized. I don't remember much about her, but I do remember that she and my great-grandfather lived in a large, old house on South High Street in my hometown. I also remember she was the first person I ever visited in the hospital. On Christmas morning I awoke ridiculously early, roused my brother and sister out of their beds, and then woke my parents so we could go downstairs and open presents. We were in the midst of tearing off wrapping paper and playing with new toys when the telephone rang. You can guess the news: my great-grandmother Edith had died on Christmas morning.

I distinctly remember a couple of things about that day. It was the first time I remember seeing my dad cry. His sadness and grief were palpable for a few minutes. Everything in the house stopped, and my mother moved toward him and put her arms around his shoulders. Then I remember something else; he said we had no reason not to go ahead and enjoy the day. I don't know how we managed it, but Christmas turned out to be enjoyable and fun (the norm in our family), in no way ruined by this sad news. I'm sure Dad was grieving more than he let on to us kids.

I still carry the lesson of that Christmas with me. In one way or another I use it each year. Christmas doesn't have to be perfect. Christ wants to be born each year on Christmas Day, especially on those days that turn out to be less than what we had hoped. I love W. H. Auden's poetic line, "if there when Grace dances, / I should dance."[21]

Christmas day is about the arrival of grace. It's the story of God drawing near, the God we identify with words such as *love* and *grace* and *joy*—words that coalesce in the person of Jesus Christ. Most of us

---

[21]W. H. Auden, "Whitsunday in Kirchstetten," in *A Christmas Sourcebook* (Chicago: Liturgy Training Publications, 1984), 53.

want something to change in our worlds. We want this improved or that resolved. We want the many pieces of our living to come together so we can be happy. But when grace arrives, we should dance! Even if all is not right; even if some of the pieces are still missing.

Christmas is the story of God becoming flesh. But what does such a notion mean for us? The mystery of the incarnation can be understood in a variety of ways, but at least one meaning is that God can be found in the living now of each day. Christ is born *this* day.

Yes, he was born centuries ago in Bethlehem. It's a lovely nativity story replete with stars and angels, shepherds and magi. But today he is born into our experience, into our feelings, thoughts, and situations. Therefore, this Christmas Day may be perfectly choreographed for you with decorations, gifts, and friends. Or this Christmas Day you may experience a lonely time of nostalgia and sadness. Maybe this Christmas Day is full of ambiguity for you—a mixture of joy and sorrow, frivolity and pensiveness. Regardless of the circumstances of the day, grace arrives on Christmas morning. If grace arrives, then surely the best thing we can do is dance.

Not long ago, I read a story by Reynolds Price about a Christmas Day he spent in Rome as a lonely graduate student. Spending Christmas in a great city such as Rome may sound thrilling, but he was twenty-two years old and away from home for the first time. For him it really wasn't thrilling at all. He was homesick, sitting on a bench outside the Colosseum feeling sorry for himself. Then something happened. Though almost fifty years have passed since that Christmas in Rome, Price remembers it with vividness and gratitude:

> A young woman, maybe my age, in a tan dress, a coarse brown shawl on her hair and shoulders, one hand on the child beside her—a boy with filthy knees and a coat so tattered it hung in comical strips. Was he five years old or older? They were beggars surely but—no—their hands didn't reach out toward me, though their black eyes never flinched from my face...I knew I had a handful of change...but before I brought it out to

daylight…the woman shook her head once—No. She gave the boy a gentle push forward…They were selling souvenirs, like fakes. I smiled, "No grazie," holding both my hands out empty…but the boy reached up and laid the coin on my right palm.

I'd spent hours with a boyhood coin box; and when I turned the bronze coin over, I knew it was real with the profile of one of the saner Caesars, Hadrian—worth maybe fifteen dollars. I still didn't need it and offered it back. But the child wasn't selling. He returned and trotted off to his mother…she launched a smile of amazing light at me and said what amounted to, "You, for you. The coin is for you."

I still have the coin.[22]

On this Christmas Day, wherever you may be and whatever may unfold for you and your family, I encourage you to trust this: *grace arrives!* Christ was born to love us, and we were born to receive his love. All we can do is open our hands on Christmas Day and receive the goodness of God's presence. God is with us. Perhaps we clutch the gifts of this day like a coin in the palm of our hand. Or maybe, if you are so inclined, you might even consider dancing, because when grace arrives, all we can really do is dance.

I greet you this Christmas Day, O God, and I am thankful for the child born so long ago. I think of others in the world this day. Some celebrate Christmas alone. Some celebrate Christmas hungry. Some are torn apart by war and violence. Some will open no gifts at all. I ask for Christ to be born in me, not simply for my comfort and peace, but for the comfort and peace of all your children. Amen.

---

[22]Reynolds Price, *Feasting the Heart* (New York: Scribner, 200), 13–14.

The Winter Brings Spring

SECTION FIVE

DECEMBER 26

Finding Your Sacred Space

I was glad when they said to me, / "Let us go to the house of the LORD!"

PSALM 122:1

Much like classical music and ballet, sacred space seems to be in a perilous tailspin these days. Many churches are implementing "contemporary" styles of worship. That often means utilizing casual places such as fellowship halls or bland auditoriums for worship services. However, I still think it's worth discovering (and for some, rediscovering) the value of encountering God within sacred space.

I fully believe God can be found in the beautiful sunrise while hiking in the mountains, or the stunning sunset while strolling on the beach. But I also think certain places built expressly for the purpose of understanding the gospel are infused with mystery and meaning. When we enter them, we know we are in the presence of God. Rather than running from our churches during our times of spiritual winter (a phenomenon that is all too common), we should seek out these spaces and places because the architecture itself can provide healing and insight for our lives.

I have followed with keen interest the past few years the construction project of Our Lady of the Angels Cathedral in Los Angeles, California. This new cathedral has cost a staggering $189 million and has raised all kinds of questions from both Catholics and non-Catholics alike. Some of these questions include: How can the church spend this kind of money on a building when so much human need plagues the world? Is a building such as this an obscene demonstration of power and wealth, given what we know about the simple life of Jesus?

I've had the privilege of seeing some of the most beautiful sacred spaces in the world. In their own unique way, they have become important to my soul. I have great affinity for Riverside Church in New York City, partly because I love the church and the senior minister, James Forbes, but partly because the space itself invites me to think and feel and experience God in a new way. I could say the same about Grace Cathedral in San Francisco. I never travel to San Francisco without taking time to sit in its lovely nave or walk the labyrinth that sets atop Nob Hill. I have also had the opportunity to worship in Notre Dame of Paris and visit Saint Chappele a few blocks away.

All these spaces, of course, are extraordinary in and of themselves. All of them are a far cry from the simple manger in which the baby Jesus was born. Nevertheless, it seems to me that sacred space has its place in the life of faith. These spaces can become temporary homes for our religious sensibilities and longings, our need for quiet, grandeur, reverence, and mystery. As human beings we seem to be wired, not only for religious experience, but also to honor and treasure that experience through the imagination of architecture. In ancient Judaism, for example, architecture may have been as primitive as mounding some dirt and stacking a pile of rocks to mark an encounter with the Divine. It could also be as elaborate as Solomon's temple. Regardless, the capacity to experience God includes the impetus to mark the occasion and remember the place as holy.

In the case of churches, the gospel is not merely preached with words a minister delivers. The sublime dimensions of art and color and architecture also communicate the gospel. Viewed from one perspective, many things about a church building seem impractical and superfluous. This is true of Saint Peter's in Rome as well as the county seat churches dotting the American landscape. Yet the superfluous parts of the building are the very parts I find myself treasuring the most—crosses and candles, lecterns and vaulted ceilings, art and stained glass windows. They remind me that I am in a different space, that I am in this space to encounter the divine presence. Church buildings tap into something deeper than steel beams and concrete, bricks and mortar. To walk into sacred space is to experience the ineffable that beats within the heart of the universe, as well as in our own humanity.

I'll never forget the candlelight memorial service we held at University Christian Church after the September 11 tragedy. The sanctuary was dimly lit. Hundreds of people offered their prayers to God. We sang. We were silent. We wept and held one another. Someone came up to me after the service and said, "I don't want you to take this wrong, because I liked your sermon and thought the music was wonderful, but most of all, I just wanted to be here. I wanted to sit in this space instead of being alone in my living room watching television. I just wanted to be in a place where I could feel close to God."

That's the power of sacred space. It transcends utilitarianism and flies in the face of practicality. Sacred space can be found in a great cathedral or local church sanctuary, because the space takes on a life of its own, and, therefore, has the power to give us life when we need it most.

This is why during the Advent season I would encourage you to reacquaint yourself with sacred space. If you haven't been to church in a while, make sure you attend. (You don't have to wait until next Christmas!) Maybe just as important, stop by a church during the week so you can quietly sit in the sanctuary for a few minutes. Listen to the silence. Listen to your own heart beating, your feelings gently falling to the floor like feathers. Pray to God, and listen for the Spirit. Pay attention to the architecture. Notice the wood. The colors. The smells. You'll find something extraordinarily special, something lovely and beautiful, and yes, something wonderfully sacred that will make a difference in your celebration of Christmas.

Living God, I know I can find you anywhere and anytime. Yet, dearest God, I have found you in sacred places of worship again and again, in cathedrals great and chapels small. During this season of preparing my heart for the birth of Jesus, may my soul become a quiet manger in which he can be born and a magnificent cathedral in which we might live forever. Amen.

DECEMBER 27

Building a Life Worth Remembering

When they saw this, they made known what had been told them about this child.

LUKE 2:17

The irony was too much to ignore. On the morning of July 24, 2002, two juxtaposed obituaries appeared in virtually every major newspaper across the country. Both men were writers and left behind a considerable number of admirers. Both men died of cancer. Yet that's where the similarity ends.

One headline read: *William Pierce, 69, Neo-Nazi Leader and Author, Is Dead.* Across the page the other simply stated: *Chaim Potok, Who Illumined the World of Hasidic Judaism, Dies at 73.*[23] Two deaths. Two obituaries. Two dramatically different lives.

---

[23]David Cay Johnson, "William Pierce, 69, Neo-Nazi Leader, Dies," *The New York Times,* 24 July 2002, 16; Margalite Fox, "Chaim Potok, 73, Dies; Novelist Illuminated the World of Hasidic Judaism, *The New York Times,* 24 July 2002, 17.

I had never heard of William Pierce until the trial of Timothy McVeigh, convicted of bombing the Murrah Federal Building in Oklahoma City. McVeigh claimed that one of his inspirations for carrying out this heinous act of violence was Pierce's book *The Turner Diaries*. Pierce was a neo-Nazi, a purveyor of white supremacist literature, and an ardent anti-Semite. Although well-educated with degrees from Rice University and the University of Colorado, he nevertheless used his education to defame anyone who was not of white European descent. What distinguished his life was not a career in physics (his field of expertise), but forty years of writing that inflamed hatred and fear. His book *Hunter*, the story of a man who hunts down and kills interracial couples, sold more than a half million copies. Pierce also established a publishing company that became the largest seller of hate literature and music within the United States.

Chaim Potok was an ordained rabbi and scholar, primarily known as a novelist of extraordinary depth and insight. I vividly remember reading his book *The Chosen*, a story of a young man wrestling with his strict Hasidic faith and the inner turmoil he felt because of a desire to participate in secular culture. The struggle between faith and culture was a consistent theme for Potok. He understood that faith could both nurture and negate life, alternately becoming liberating and oppressive to the human soul.

In *My Name Is Asher Lev*, Potok portrayed a Jewish artist who courageously painted scenes of crucifixion, or, just as appalling to his strict family, scenes of nude women. The tension between artistic integrity and respect for the traditions of Judaism was a centerpiece in all of Potok's literature. In yet another novel, *The Beginning*, the protagonist implements the use of modern, critical scholarship while interpreting scripture. Such an approach created enormous inner turmoil as well as testing the boundaries of a faith community who affirmed the literal truth of their sacred writings.

What strikes me about each of these obituaries is not what either man finally wrote or ultimately accomplished, but that they would be featured side-by-side in death. These two men represented polar opposites in the force of their humanity. Both recognized the contradictions and inconsistencies of life, and both grappled with a dynamic, changing world. Potok, however, sought to be a redemptive voice for humanity. Instead of cursing the darkness of his world, he brought light and insight, not offering easy answers, but telling stories that illumined the lives of his readers.

Pierce, on the other hand, created a much different trajectory for his life. Rather than bringing light to the world, he became small-minded and hateful. Protectionist in his view of race and nation, he consistently threw gasoline on the sparks of suspicion and xenophobia. Hatred and bigotry, whether they are organized around race or religion, are always dangerous. Yet they become even more volatile when someone like Pierce tries to disguise them in intellectual social theory or revisionist history.

The fact that these men could build two diametrically opposed lives remains one of the great mysteries of the human experience. In the end, we are free, dangerously free. Part of what happens during the Advent season is that we have the chance to contemplate that freedom by becoming more aware of our choices and values. With our freedom we are able to love or hate, help or hurt. We are free to lift up our neighbor who has fallen or to choose to grind him more deeply into the ground. We make these choices daily. Every now and then one notable act of courage distinguishes our lives; but more routinely, the imperceptible ways we treat others finally compose the essence of our lives. Over the course of any given day, we accumulate words, actions, and attitudes.

As I reflected on these two oddly juxtaposed obituaries, I could not help but think that each of these men had become a kind of book, a life spelled out for the world to read and judge. The dissonance between the two, of course, speaks volumes, reminding us that the life we build is also a manuscript that will be read.

Advent is not a time to over-read and scrutinize ourselves unrealistically. Too much of that has been done in the name of Christian faith, often ending in unnecessary shame or insufferable self-righteousness.

Advent is an invitation to consider who we are; what we do, say, and feel, and, finally, what is being spelled out through us day after day. You are a book, spelled out to your friends and family and world. What is being read through you today? What will finally be remembered?

What do people see when they read my life, dear God? What story draws them in? What language inspires or turns them away? Write your story upon my heart, O God, and help me become the kind of person who embodies an energy and beauty not of my own, but of the Christ who was born in Bethlehem so long ago. Amen.

DECEMBER 28

A Little Vision Goes a Long Way

"Where there is no vision, the people perish."

PROVERBS 29:18, KJV

A few years ago, I spoke at an annual breakfast for ministers and chaplains at Sparks Regional Hospital in Fort Smith, Arkansas. While there, I learned how the hospital was founded. Back in the 1800s, Arkansas didn't have a hospital. The people in Fort Smith had talked about it and knew they needed one, but interestingly enough, the physicians could never agree on what kind of hospital it should be. So, as often is the case, nothing was done for the community.

One day a man working on the railroad near Fort Smith had his leg badly mangled in heavy machinery. A doctor soon recognized that the man needed extensive medical care. The physician ran to town and told Father George Degen, an Episcopal priest, about the man's accident. Father Degen became both passionate and angry. He said to the doctor, "We've been talking about this long enough; we need a hospital, and we need it today!"

Father Degen literally walked up and down the streets of Fort Smith talking to all the merchants, describing the man's accident, and insisting that as responsible citizens they had no choice but to donate money for a hospital. By the end of the day, he had raised $500 (a considerable sum at that time) and had rented the only available house in town to use as a hospital. Women in his church gathered used furniture and brought it to the house. They also donated linens and supplies from their own homes. A cook was hired. That afternoon the injured railroad worker was moved into the first hospital in the state of Arkansas. Sparks Regional Hospital was born that day out of human need and courageous vision. It now serves thousands of patients each year in that little corner of the state.

Isn't it amazing how a little vision can change the world? Someone such as Elie Wiesel, for example, endured the horrors of the Holocaust, but emerged to give voice to grief and hope like no one else in his generation. Nelson Mandela, imprisoned for years in South Africa, never relinquished his hope for a better nation. When apartheid was finally dismantled, he was freely elected to serve as president. Jane Goodall did her work as an obscure scientist with the chimpanzee population of Tanzania. From her keen observations of these remarkable creatures, she has forged a much larger ecological vision for the well-being of the planet.

The world is changed again and again when people dare to imagine what's possible. The writer of the book of Proverbs states it like this: "Where there is no vision, the people perish" (Prov. 29:18 KJV). Part of the winter experience is taking time to imagine what is possible, moreover, to imagine a different kind of world for ourselves and others. New visions for life often emerge in those places that feel the most desolate and empty. Necessity may be the mother of invention, but winter is often the catalyst for new vision!

I can't help but wonder: Is there some vision for your life that is growing, perhaps becoming clearer during this Christmas season? Is there some possibility for your church or community that you have been pondering, but now, during this season of spiritual renewal, you know it is time to act upon it?

The movie *The Shipping News* portrays a family who has experienced the devastating loss of their house in a horrific storm. As they look at the vacant lot where their house once stood, one of their children (sometimes children lead us out of our winters) captures the moment beautifully with her innocent remark, "At least we have a view we never knew we had."[24]

Many times we find ourselves in the midst of winter experiences, not because we have done anything wrong or because anything wrong has been done to us. Sometimes we are in winter because we have ignored some of the deepest longings of our own hearts. I have sometimes wondered if our souls in some way don't constellate our winters, just so we can discover a deeper wisdom for our lives. The soul, after all, will not be ignored! Perhaps it's the accountant who experiences a crisis because he always wanted to be a teacher. Maybe it's the executive who always wanted to be an artist, or the attorney who longs to attend seminary and become a minister. Maybe it's the businesswoman who holds a longtime dream of starting her own company.

We can't do everything in life. Choices have to be made. Along the way we eventually compromise some of our dreams and aspirations. That's part of living. At the same time, it's essential that we become aware of some of the deepest hopes within us, whether they are for ourselves, the larger world, or in some cases, both. To find the equivalent of our Father Degen experience (having a vision and making a different world) is essential to our spiritual lives.

During this season as we bask in the glow of Christmas, I think it's especially important to remember that in the birth of Jesus Christ a vision was released into the world—a vision of compassion and grace; of love, mercy, and action. Of course, December is a time of tinsel and

---

[24]*The Shipping News*, directed by Lasse Hallstron, with Kevin Spacey and Julianne Moore (Miramax, 2002).

decoration, parties, and now cleaning up after the big day. But beyond all that pretends to be Christmas, we have an opportunity to believe something new is possible for our world. Vision has always changed the world, primarily because it first and foremost changes us.

Living God, become my vision for life. Forgive me when I turn away from the possible because I am afraid of it or because I have become attached to the status quo of living. I pray that the vision of Jesus Christ, a vision of hope and love for this world, will continue to transform me so that I might become an instrument of change for your creation. Amen.

DECEMBER 29

Being Yourself and Letting Others Do the Same

> *Jesus increased in wisdom and in years, and in divine and human favor.*
>
> LUKE 2:52

The gift of divine love not only touches our soul, it gives us permission to live into our truest self. Unfortunately, some have interpreted the Christian message as the call to become something different than what they are—a "new person in Christ" is the language often used. I tend to think of it a little differently. Conversion is not so much changing ourselves (though I understand the need for making life changes); it is really the opportunity to become who we *are*, finding the courage to be the people God created us to be.

Divine love excavates the deepest self from our lives. It's as if the deepest "you" within you and the deepest "me" within me is a golden ball. The golden ball was dropped into a deep and murky lake. It has become covered with mud and moss, twigs and debris. But divine love pulls it up, ever so slowly lifting it from the depths. Then divine love cleans it off and polishes it up until finally the true gold and beauty of what God created us to be is rediscovered. Sometimes this golden self is spoken of as the "inner child," or even the "little Christ" within us all. This is why we resonate so much with the celebration of Christmas. We see the beauty of the Christ child; but in reality, it is our own childlike beauty we are trying to discover.

I thought about this after the publication of Richard Chamberlain's autobiography.[25] Chamberlain began his acting career by starring in a weekly television show entitled *Dr. Kildare*. Chamberlain portrayed a young doctor who was the perfect combination of compassion and intelligence. In each weekly episode, Dr. Kildare would carefully diagnose the illnesses of his patients and treat them accordingly. In fact, he treated them so well that they all seemed to recover by the end of each hour-long episode!

Unlike most celebrities, Chamberlain actually took time to write this book himself. And well he should! In addition to writing about his outstanding career as an actor, he also shares his personal story of being a gay man. For decades he sought to keep his sexual orientation private. He was afraid of recrimination in the Hollywood film industry, afraid of losing his viability as a "leading man" in television and movies, and also afraid of what some of his closest friends might think. In his poignant autobiography, Chamberlain found the courage not only to be honest about his sexual orientation but also to reveal that he has quietly shared his life with a committed, long-term partner.

I can only begin to imagine the private pain Chamberlain endured throughout most of his adult life. Because of his handsome good looks, he was the ideal candidate for a romantic lead in a film. Yet if people had known he was gay, chances were that most of those leading roles would have been offered to someone else. His story is just another

---

[25]Richard Chamberlain, *Shattered Love: A Memoir* (New York: HarperCollins, 2003).

reminder of how hard it is for men and women, particularly gay people, to come forward and honestly say that this is who I am, this is what I feel, and this is where my life is going.

In my estimation, everyone deserves to recover the golden ball of their true selves. Sadly, gay people's fears of judgment are not without warrant. What is especially disturbing is to see how religion is often used as a justification for condemning gays and lesbians. Many times, men and women who have come to terms with their sexual orientation, often an agonizing process in and of itself, have not only experienced judgment from confused family members and friends, they have also felt the bitter sting of being pushed away from their communities of faith.

To be sure, those who read the Bible in a literal way conclude that God condemns homosexuality. Others (and I count myself as one of them) recognize that, during the time when the Bible was written, no one really conceived of someone "being" a homosexual in any psychological and physiological sense. What is condemned is not so much one "being" a homosexual, but acts of homosexual (and heterosexual) violence that harm the personhood of another individual. What God wants within all intimate relationships is integrity and love.

Admittedly this is a complex topic. Still, it seems to me that even *if* the Bible condemned homosexuality, it would still be reprehensible for anyone to treat a gay or lesbian person with anything less than dignity and respect. Not only did Jesus call upon people to love their neighbors, but to do so *especially* when our neighbor is different from us. Frequently, families are the ones who have to come to terms with this issue in a personal way. This occurs when a parent, for example, or a child or relative finally shares that he or she is gay. Yet I'm inspired at how families continue to love that person, neither *because of* nor *in spite of* their sexual orientation, but because of their qualities as a human being.

Bigotry is always ghastly, but never more so than when it is practiced in God's name. If the beauty of the Christ child is to work its transforming power in our lives during this season of Christmas, then surely one way it does so is by helping each of us discover the most true, most authentic, most real person within us. Maybe it won't be something as dramatic as our sexual orientation, but in ways great and small, Christ invites us to rediscover our inner gold. It always takes faith. But, after all, isn't that what this season is all about?

Moreover, Christmas is a season not only to discover the grace of being ourselves, but also to extend that grace to others as they try to become themselves. I am still contemplating that baby born in Bethlehem, but what I know is this: He grew and became a man who possessed the courage to be the person God created him to be. He shared grace so that others could do the same. This isn't just the spirit of Christmas; it is the reality of Christ.

Loving God, I thank you for giving me the gift of Christ: not a little god walking around among mortals, but true humanity, true flesh luminous with divine presence. Even as Jesus found the courage to become himself, give me that same courage, and then give me the capacity to love and accept others. Amen.

DECEMBER 30

The Gifts We Bring

In all this I have given you an example that by such work we must support the weak, remembering the words of the Lord Jesus, for he himself said, "It is more blessed to give than to receive."

ACTS 20:35

No matter how often ministers pontificate from the pulpit about the commercialization of Christmas and the evil of materialism lurking behind every present purchased during December, people will still give and receive gifts during the holidays. Well they should, because one of the most poignant moments in the Christmas story involves the magi presenting their gifts to the Christ child.

Not much is known about the magi—who they were, or what their motives were when they presented their gold, frankincense, and myrrh. Yet who they were historically is not nearly as important as what they represent poetically in the story of the first Christmas.

You seldom experience a more moving moment than when someone presents you with a gift expressing love. And what is more atisfying than when you give someone a present, one that is not ontrived or dictated by a date on the calendar, but given out of pure enerosity? Fortunately I've been on both sides of the giving equation, nd I would have to say that they are equally delicious.

I have received certain gifts that have practically moved me to ears—a pair of cufflinks from a friend, help with sabbatical expenses rom a church family, and a surprise round of golf at Pebble Beach my amily presented me for Father's Day several years ago. When I give ;ifts, I tend to offer something that holds meaning for me. Rather than rying to calculate what the other person wants or needs, I like to give ;ifts that become a footnote from my own heart. Consequently, I have ;iven countless volumes of poetry to friends because poetry has been he oxygen of my spiritual life. I have presented musical CDs that have iurtured me. Lately, I've been giving movies to people, films that I iave loved over the years.

It seems important to highlight another kind of gift during this eason of giving and receiving. It's the momentous gift of our humanity o one another. Every person we meet offers us something. Sometimes vhat they offer is clear and obvious, such as a teacher who brings knowledge to the classroom, or a physician who prescribes medicine that will cure us. We are grateful for the gifts these people bring to us, ind we celebrate their presence as a manifestation of God's love.

All the while we receive less obvious gifts each day, gifts that require a deeper kind of seeing and receiving. At the times I have received them, I have not always appreciated the gifts someone might be giving me. Only later, after more experience and growing, could I look back and recognize the subtle gifts of life a person was presenting me.

My friend Ken Lawrence brings me the gift of enthusiasm over a piece of art. My friend Diane Zehr gives me the gift of unconditional love and listening. My son Matthew brings me the gift of language. My colleague Cyndy Twedell brings me the gift of compassion. My father gives me the gift of unswerving love. The list could go on and on, but in some ways my life has become a thrift store of experience— each person I meet making a distinctive contribution to my life.

If Christmas could work its magic on us this year, then surely one result would be to increase our capacity to discern and receive the gifts of others. This sometimes requires us to let go of our expectations and inhibitions. A good question to ask is: "What inhibits my recognizing and receiving the gifts of others?"

We have to let go of our need to have other people agree with us. If we only see virtue in those who agree with us, what we wind up seeing becomes terribly narrow and small.

We have to stop requiring other people to become like us before they have any value in the world. The word *diversity* has almost become a cliché these days, but diversity and differences can enhance life and enlarge our experience.

We have to relinquish our need to judge others if we are to receive their gifts. We may not like everything about the other person, and in some cases, we might disagree with what a person believes or has done, but that doesn't mean we can't receive the gifts that person possesses.

To receive the gifts of others, we have to let go of our need for perfection. No one in the world is perfect for us—not our children, not our spouses, not our friends. However, just because a person may not be everything to us, that doesn't mean that person can't bring something to our lives.

We have to let go of self-sufficiency to be nurtured by the gifts of others. Some of us think it is a sign of weakness to need something from someone. Why is it a weakness to need another person? To take responsibility for ourselves is always good, but that doesn't mean we don't need others.

Of course, giving gifts has two sides. Just as we can get in the way of receiving gifts, we can also get in the way when it comes to giving them. Maybe some of us don't think we have gifts to give. Perhaps we think our gifts don't matter. Maybe we've been rejected and can't bear the thought of being pushed away one more time. Sometimes we become too grandiose about our gifts, thinking that we don't want to "waste" them on people who will not understand.

I want to believe that no gift offered is ever a wasted gift. When we take time to offer ourselves to the world—our love, our creativity, our compassion—someone finally receives our gift. If the Christmas story can ring true inside our hearts as we prepare to begin a new year, then surely we are right in believing that Christ always receives our gifts. At last, the one sent for us as the perfect gift also becomes the perfect receiver of all that we offer the world.

I want to give my gifts to the world, dear God, but not always for the right reasons. Sometimes I want someone to say, "How wonderful you are! How generous you are!" But in my best moments what I aspire is this: To be myself, to share my thoughts, my feelings, my hopes, my dreams. I trust that it is enough. I want to receive gifts, too—love and friendship and genuine communication. Help me to open my heart so that I might receive the many gifts you present each day. Amen.

DECEMBER 31

Giving the Heart Its Time

> *"But the tax collector, standing far off, would not even look up to heaven, but was beating his breast and saying, 'God, be merciful to me, a sinner!'"*

Luke 18:13

The British physician William Harvey published a groundbreaking essay in 1628 describing the human heart as a circulatory pump. Think about that for a moment—the heart as a pump, as a machine with mechanical function! It would be hard to overstate the significance this metaphor has had on our self-understanding as human beings. Harvey, always possessing a flair for the dramatic, would often hold aloft a human heart in his bare hands (no doubt excised from the chest of an expired criminal) for everyone to see. He would then proclaim, "This is your heart! This is the pump that keeps you alive."[26]

In effect, Harvey demythologized the heart. No longer would the heart be a mystical place of emotion and poetry and music. Certainly it

---

[26]Gail Godwin, *Heart* (HarperCollins, 2001), 112.

would not be regarded as the center of religious experience. A scientific coup seized and made captive the heart, even to the point that in contemporary culture if you cannot prove something to be true scientifically, then most of us think it must not be true at all. In many ways, the paradigm of science has hijacked the human experience of mystery and faith.

Yet something in our humanity pushes against the notion that everything must be explained scientifically. If the season of Advent and Christmas has touched us at all, then it has surely deepened our humanity and awakened our hearts. We are more than molecules, cells, and organs; more than medicines and surgeries. The heart in all its metaphoric beauty suggests we have the capacity for depth. But what is depth? I think our wondrous ability to think, to feel, to love and suffer, and then to love again is part of our depth. Depth is the totality of our existence, and, yes, depth is the territory of the Divine.

A loved one dies, and a family gathers at a funeral home. They huddle around the casket and vacuously gaze at the body. Someone may say, "Oh, doesn't he look nice." "He looks so natural." Yet there's a deeper truth longing to be heard. A child articulated this truth several years ago after seeing her grandfather in a casket. The little girl blurted out, "Grandpa isn't in there anymore, is he?" No, he isn't. Something is missing. That something missing is nothing less than heart energy.

Here we are on the brink of a new year, the last day of December. Christmas is past, but like much of life, winter lingers. What would it be like to live with a new sense of heart this year? Maybe what I'm thinking about is discovering an *enlightened* heart. Enlightenment isn't a destination, nor is it something we achieve. It's not about progress or about getting better. The enlightened heart is about moving closer to our essence as men and women, faithfully moving toward that sacred place where the presence of Christ is born and lives.

The notable people I admire most have journeyed toward their own center only to find something other than their own egos filling it. C. S. Lewis, a professor and writer in England and a complete rationalist, would have agreed with Harvey's essay on the heart! But Lewis found himself surprised by God and became a Christian. More than that, he found himself surprised by the sweetness of love with a woman. A confirmed bachelor, he eventually married and stood beside her as she suffered and died of cancer. Lewis did not see his conversion to Christianity as leading him away from reality. On the contrary, the love of Christ brought him home to the reality of his own heart.

Thomas Merton was studying at Columbia University in New York City, a lost, bewildered young man. A few years later, not unlike C. S. Lewis, he found himself surprised by God. He moved to a monastery in the rolling hills of Kentucky. At long last Merton found the home he had been searching for most of his life. His movement toward the Christian faith was intellectual, to be sure, but for Merton, his conversion to Christ meant coming home to the beauty of his own heart.

Dorothy Day was a young woman; yet her life had been nothing but one hardship after another. She was lost and unhappy. Seemingly nothing she did grounded her life in any kind of reality. She had started her writing career at an early age, but something was missing. She wanted and needed something more than her early success as an author. She made her way to a little church called St. Joseph's in New York, sat on the back pew alone, and prayed. She stopped by the church to enjoy the quiet reflections of her heart. Then one day she prayed the prayer, "God be merciful to me, a sinner." Her life began to change. For the first time she found something of worth and value within her. She wrote more books throughout her life, but primarily she became known as the woman with a keen mind and big heart who helped the poor and attended to the needs of the oppressed and hungry.[27]

There's no easy way out of winter. As I have tried to suggest, getting out of our winter isn't the point anyway. On a day when we ring out the old and ring in the new, our hearts await our attention. What is missing inside your life? What will you move toward in this upcoming year? What are you doing with the energy of your heart?

---

[27]Paul Elie, *The Life You Save May Be Your Own: An American Pilgrimage* (New York: Farrar, Straus, and Giroux, 2003).

Christ wants to live in only one place, the place where his vision for becoming a whole and real person is made true. That is the place of the human heart. Make this new year a time of giving attention to your heart, perhaps giving your heart back to itself. No matter how restless or barren we may feel, God is searching for us, searching for our hearts. The truth of the matter is God is as homesick for us as we are for God.

That, of course, is the winter name of God.

God of new beginnings, I end this year with so many feelings. I have had shortcomings and failures. I have made mistakes. I have had some successes, too. I ask, however, that this not be a day of endings, but a moment of new beginnings. Give me courage to open my heart to you and others. I bless you this day and thank you for the Christ child. May the depths of my heart become his home even as my home becomes his presence for others. Amen.